Anthony Johnson: Committed for murder.

Martin Williams

chipmunkapublishing
the mental health publisher

Martin Williams

All rights reserved, no part of this publication may be reproduced by any means, electronic, mechanical photocopying, documentary, film or in any other format without prior written permission of the publisher.

> Published by
> Chipmunkapublishing
> United Kingdom

http://www.chipmunkapublishing.com

Copyright © Martin Williams 2017

ISBN   978-1-78382-388-8

Anthony Johnson

Anthony Johnson: Committed for murder.

Anthony Johnson woke early, the weather for June was not really any better than it had been of late, dismal. Silencing his alarm clock, an arm protruded from under the covers and he set the snooze button. It rang a second time, just as he was dosing off, but this time his whole body sprang into action. Desperately trying to compose himself, he stood at the top of the stairs, where he had made a mental note of the mail and accompanying newspaper. Later, after he had washed, shaved and dressed, he sat down at the kitchen table, the newspaper open, he devoured a bowl of cornflakes. It was the usual unfortunate and unlikely reports that generally took him longest to read.

The mail, one envelope, white and probably from the bank, the other to Anthony's mind a lovely little brown envelope that might mean money. Both stood propped up against an empty toast rack.

The cornflakes finished he swilled the bowl round and put it and the spoon on the drying rack. First the white envelope, as he had surmised it was from the bank. Alright, nothing to worry about there, his account was in credit even if he wasn't rich. The brown envelope then, also as he had imagined. A giro for three hundred and ninety pounds and sixty pence, arrears. He couldn't cash it at the post office, however he could pay it into his bank account. It was just about the right amount, that isn't to say he wouldn't have liked more, but then in the same breath it wasn't so much that he would have qualms about spending it.

Thinking ahead, he wondered if he'd have enough money to get away on. The rent would need paying but he had that in his weekly payment, it wasn't anybodies birthday and quite frankly he found himself juggling with at home or abroad.

Abroad posed certain problems of its own, he would need travellers cheques and foreign currency, but that wasn't so much of a worry, he could go to any travel agent and get what he needed. But if he went abroad it would probably mean, in the long run, he would be more likely to spend more. However a holiday here at home could also be expensive. He could cut costs though by taking a tent or staying in a youth hostel. It would have to wait, he couldn't decide there and then.

Putting the cheque in what was neither a waist coat or a body warmer, but somewhere in between (what he lovingly called his shooting jacket although it had no arms). He patted his pocket, checked he had his keys, and went out of the same door by which the mail had come an hour earlier.

This sleeveless jacket, which boasted zips and pockets all over, also boasted a hood, which Anthony would sometimes wear. It covered his walkman head set which relayed music from the tape part which was secured to his belt. The tapes for this machine ranged from Beethoven to Bach and from Level 42 to Dire Straits, in fact in some respects Anthony's tastes could be said to be catholic.

Arriving at the bus stop, he immediately took note of the fact that there was no-one else on the bus stop, which generally meant that one had to wait longer, but with both city and country buses available one was never sure. Five minutes, half an hour, one was as possible as the other. In fact this morning Anthony's luck was in, he waited five or ten minutes no longer. His preferred seat was downstairs preferably opposite the stair well where one could watch the ladies legs as they went upstairs for a seat. But this seat having been taken he would sit right at the back, where even an encounter was not impossible.

As luck would have it today he had the seat opposite the stair well but with no particular reason he soon lost interest. Wasn't it a pity young women wore trousers he had mused, but then that served him right did it not.

One would have thought that faced with spending the day on his own Anthony would have welcomed a friendly face getting on the bus, but no. Not given to idle chit chat Anthony welcomed the anonymity of being on a crowded bus amidst the throng of passengers making their way to the centre of town. The semi-detached houses soon made way for high rise flats and then just a few minutes further one was in the centre.

Anthony stepped off the bus outside a large retail store and retraced the journey for a block and there was his bank; with a few minutes to spare before it opened there was a small queue. It occurred to Anthony that he could go for a coffee and come back later, after all he had all day, but with so few minutes to wait before it opened he decided to sit it out. When it opened he went straight upstairs where the cash was dispensing and filling in both a paying in slip and a paying out, he left the bank a few moments later with thirty pounds in his pocket.

Heading for one of those rather expensive foreign type of cafes he passed the shoe repair and key cutting shop and made a mental note that in all probability he expected to forget to bring in his shoes. Once at the cafe he ordered an expresso which he took very sweet almost like a Greek coffee.

Frankly an expresso didn't take that long to drink, but unlike Anthony, a lot of people in a similar position to him didn't really start their day until midday. It wasn't that he was necessarily unemployed but the doctor at one point had thought to sign him off and thus it had stayed. In every way this suited Anthony who had the presence of mind to indulge fully in life away from the constraints of a nine to five job; and receiving a state pension he was able to manage without allowing himself to spiral into debt.

Without giving any further details it may be said of Anthony he was fairly well fixed; given that his overheads were small, he lived a life which he himself thought of as recumbent. A wife (well one is bound to ask), no Anthony had no wife, although to be fair Anthony enjoyed the pleasures of the opposite sex both in and out of bed.

Looking at his watch, he reassured himself, for he already

knew that it was a little after ten thirty. Today, although he had been pleased to receive his bonus, was not one of those days that Anthony had a great deal to do. He might spend the afternoon or at least part of it shopping for groceries and if he didn't eat in town he would probably need some meat for that evening, although as often as not he would eat in a cafe or one of the large department stores, and would then only have a light snack in the evening; he would buy his meat at the butchers being some what dubious about that that was sold in the supermarket.

At times Anthony felt quite paranoid about being in town, sometimes fantasizing that someone was watching him; further to this he liked to imagine that he was going to steal something expensive and to that end he loved looking in jewellers, although he knew all to well this was a dream that was so far from reality as to be considered completely impossible. And although he spent hours looking at the Rolex watches and bright diamonds he in fact knew very little of what was genuinely expensive and what was merely a passing fad. It was also like this with music, whilst he probably would have enjoyed all sorts of different things, he showed little interest beyond a few classic acts which he probably could not tell you why he liked even these.

Given this, one immediately thinks of a rather narrow minded individual, but his friends thought him anything but; perhaps unlikely, or perhaps not, depending on ones standpoint, Anthony held Christian beliefs, but that is to say something so private to him, that he himself would never of let that go about himself. Earlier in his life he had juggled with Buddhist philosophies, but this again was a very private matter on which he was unlikely to be drawn. His father who had while Anthony was growing up sang at the church and hence Anthony had attended Sunday school, had died believing in very little at all; he had gone from church goer to agnostic and almost atheist beliefs shortly before he died. Anthony's strength of belief had paradoxically gone in the other direction.

Leaving the cafe where Anthony had taken his coffee, he

proceeded to the bakers, where he bought a donut; Anthony loathed this sort of transaction; how could the bakery ever make any money when one just bought one donut; however that was not enough to stop him buying one all the same. He then went across the street to the pedestrian part of the shopping arcade and sat down to eat it. From its dismal beginnings the day had improved and Anthony could now feel the gentle warmth of the sun playing on the back of his head.

Anthony could not but help from noticing the new youth who became somehow younger and younger with the passing of every year. The latest was to dress, if anything, sharply only to spoil the overall effect by wearing cheap or not so cheap trainers which to Anthony were no more than bumped up pumps. Anthony's own fashion message in his day had been to dress in black and white; white socks, collars and cuffs, however as he had mellowed he had plumped for the relaxed fashion of the masses, denim trousers, check shirts and roomy sweaters.

But for all this Anthony regretted that if one was unemployed one automatically gave up the right to wear a suit. But a man of habit Anthony still boasted several, all of which, bar one, he had purchased, the one he had not having been given to him by his brother on returning from the States, where apparently such things are considerably cheaper.

One is tempted to say Anthony's views were, and are, erring towards the conservative; for him men wore trousers and women were able to cook, but besides these beliefs lay almost a contradiction in terms for in fact Anthony was a very good cook. It was in fact to his credit that he did cook, for many working or not relied on freezer meals that one just heated up in that luxury necessity a microwave. Perhaps it may be said though Anthony tended to cook foreign food but never the less most of it was genuinely fresh and he excelled himself with fish and shell fish.

Politically Anthony's feelings were something of a mess, what with the ending of the cold war, an unlikely hood, that in his childhood days would have been presumed to have been impossible. He felt some affinity for the protesters that were now almost commonplace outside meetings of the world bank, but not because he believed in socialism, more because he felt that industry and commerce were just buying out the earth. It was as Anthony saw it the last great scam, after all one could not avoid buying things, people naturally had to buy things to eat and have shelter, but now it seemed as if the largest world wide firms would supply anything from a handful of rice to a television, and possessions being nine tenths of the law, five or six companies did ninety percent of the business, and thus owned the world out right.

I am sure, as perhaps the reader may be too, that Anthony's view of the situation was of course not actually that simple and whilst he held views on the one hand that were left of centre, one is tempted to say of anyone living in the west that they were probably able to afford such opinions; but of course the more the thought about it the more the whole situation became confused.. Even he was forced to buy clothes at western prices, probably spending enough to keep a whole African village for a year or more. And with this in mind he had, when he was younger, thought about joining the Voluntary Service Overseas, but no sooner had he thought about it than he fell ill and it had all become impossible.

Lunchtime came and went and Anthony again made a mental note to pick up some meat before he went home that evening. I don't know whether I can explain Anthony's attitude for although he might well spend the best part of the day floating around the main shopping area calling perhaps at a cafe and then perhaps window shopping or just sitting around watching the shoppers go by, he seemed contented enough to do this; and he didn't seem to tire of it. Perhaps what he did not like was going home to his empty house. It wasn't that he wasn't at home there for he had lived at his current address sometime now.

About half past four he had picked up his meat at the butchers and was heading home on the bus, it was before the rush hour and so he found himself largely on a bus of shoppers; in the main older women and perhaps some pensioners. He looked at his watch, he hadn't had to wait long for a bus and he would be home within the hour. First things first he would fix himself a coffee then sit down and look in the paper to see what was on that evening, maybe he'd have a shower, then a little later he'd sit down to eat. Food preparation played quite an important part of Anthony's evening. He would first sit down and watch the evening news then he would cook, as a general rule he would cook more than he needed but it could all be put aside and frozen for another day. As he was cooking he would either have the radio on or perhaps a tape, he was too careful with his prize record collection to allow any possibility of it getting dirty from food stuffs, and whilst he only had a small CD collection, really the same applied. Tonight he was going to prepare Chicken Chasseur and with that in mind he had also bought a cheap bottle of red wine and whilst strickly speaking he wasn't supposed to drink, he might allow himself the one glass just to say he had tasted it. Isn't it always the case but just as he was sitting down the phone went, it was his mum. Anyone else and Anthony would have asked them to call back later but he did not for her; this was partly because he knew that would offend her and partly because her phone calls were never that long anyway. The long and the short of it was that she wanted him to come over to look at something electrical and although it didn't sound that difficult she agreed that perhaps it was better left to the weekend. In all probability it was no more than a fuse and then not a ring main fuse, just a thirteen amp socket fuse. Anyway he was to give her a bell before he came, just to be sure she was in and it was agreed that if he wanted to he might stay for a bite to eat. The call had lasted no more than a few minutes and he was soon sat down at what was a some what better supper than he had expected, everything considered. Again pop music played a part that evening and then Anthony went to bed. For a man like Anthony who didn't really exert himself at anything, he slept remarkably well barely stirring the whole night through.

One could of course pick out any particular day and describe what he had been up to and the day that I have chosen is possibly more typical than one would expect. The week over, Anthony would visit his mother's and as he had expected it was no more than a socket fuse, he found a small electrical screwdriver and had it fixed in minutes.

"Thank you for doing that," said his mum. "That's a weight off my mind. Both of my boys are good to me. And I know Mark would do more if only I asked him." There was a pause. Anthony didn't feel he could say anything. "Yes, really I'm pleased at how both of you turned out, all right I know you have been ill, but then Mark has had to work hard to get where he is now." Actually the two lads could not be more like chalk and cheese. Anthony laid off on the sick, Mark married with two kids and working for English China Clay. Anthony didn't mind being off sick as it gave him time to pursue his interest in art, music and literature, his brother had played tennis at county level and could think of nothing better than a game of golf. Anthony knew exactly what was coming - he had heard it a hundred times before.

"It's a shame you gave up playing the violin, I thought for a while you showed some promise and Mark he was very good at tennis." How these two quite separate ideas came to come in the same breath was perhaps something only Mrs. Johnson could explain.

"Well Mark was always very good at tennis. At one point I wondered just how far he would go."
"Oh, I don't think so, he was good but he wasn't outstanding."
Anthony had been put in his place. "I wondered if he would have gone to sea," he mused not really thinking of what he was saying.
"Of course your father went to sea."
"That's what I mean, I thought at one point Mark was going to follow in his footsteps." Mark was as I have said the younger brother so perhaps if anyone was going to follow in his footsteps it should have been Anthony. Although Anthony felt in some respects that his role in the family had somewhat been usurped, his brother being a far more confident and ebullient man than he, he still saw himself very much the elder.

Anthony Johnson

"He's all right now though."
"Oh yes, he's doing fine."
"Oh that's good." There was a somewhat stonier silence. Anthony and his mother would quite often communicate in this fashion, both treading on each others toes, both trying hard not to. A change of subject.

"How's David? Have you seen him this week?"
"No I haven't. But I expect I'll see him Monday." Actually David was one of the few friends that Anthony had that he had introduced to her. I don't know why but one is almost tempted to speak of the secret life of Anthony Johnson. The one thing Anthony could not abide was anyone looking into his private life. However with that one friend David, Anthony found he could be more candid, strange then that was the one friend he should introduce to her. Suffice it to say David's lips were sealed, although of course Anthony's candour would only stretch so far. Quite what Anthony was hiding he probably didn't know himself as he was as capable of rearranging events to suit himself, and so an event that had originally been dreamt up became a fact of his distant past, and events that had actually happened became lost in the annuals of his mind.

His mother was in fact a quite small woman to this day, Anthony's favourite pictures of her were those that he had growing up when she was serving porridge in the morning or cooking a fry up for tea. Immediately after her husband had died Anthony's role in the family became, at least as he saw it, very much more important. Initially she was just beside herself but as time went on she became indifferent and in some respects even morose. Anthony fearing for the worst, insisted that she see a doctor, of course at the tender age of eleven he knew nothing of depression or really adult mourning but he did know that she had taken it very badly. Partly due to her own insistence and partly due to the fact that she had known her G.P. for a very long time she managed to avoid any sort of Psychiatric care. He had perhaps asked the two most salient questions, those being, was she finding the children too much and was she still maintaining some sort of daily routine. Having answered both of these questions satisfactorily, and repeating somewhat optimistically that she could see light at the end of the tunnel, he sent her home with the proviso that if things got worse she would come back and see him again.

Slowly but surely her recovery began as she took the children on their summer holidays and time the great healer began to put distance between her and the terrible thing that had happened. True to her nature she never remarried but she was sometimes seen to sport a man either at some round table function or perhaps at a party, but inevitably nothing could really replace the love of her former spouse.

Although one might have been mistaken for thinking so; in fact neither Anthony nor his mother were what one would call the lonely type. Anthony's bosom friend David went back some ten or fifteen years and his mother had a lifelong friend in Peter. Peter had been acquainted with Derek, so it was only normal that he knew Mrs. Johnson, Derek Johnson being her former spouse. Again as so often seems to happen a more unlikely pair of friends than Derek and Peter one could not imagine. Peter was hard working studious even intellectual, Derek on the other hand was the out of doors, games orientated sort. So it was only natural that leaving school Peter would happily go off to university while Derek went to sea. Having qualified, Peter joined the Police force, his degree immediately allowing him position, whilst Derek eventually grew tired of the sea, or perhaps became more seriously interested in Dorothy who then became his wife. After Derek died, Peter found himself better known to Dorothy, though I believe she could see how and why Peter's marriage hadn't worked.

Far from being jealous of Peter, as perhaps one might expect of an eleven or twelve year old, Anthony and perhaps Mark to a lesser degree accepted Peter as what he was - a good friend of the family. Slightly daunted by the fact that he was Chief Inspector Finchley, it was never-the-less something which he could brag about to his peers, and that after the man he had loved so much had gone.

To bring you up to date Peter Finchley was now a Chief Inspector retired, and Mrs. Johnson who had returned to work after her husband had died was no longer a nurse.

Holidaying together as they did sometimes, Peter would tell the children of the mad axe man of Barclay Moor, and they lapped it up. Actually Peter's investigation of the mad axe man of Barclay Moor could not be farther from the truth if he had tried, because Mr. Finchley had been primarily concerned with the investigation of fraud and consequently was perhaps not best placed to tell the tale. However, the children enjoyed it and this pleased Peter the more so as he had not had children himself. Again Dorothy had her own opinion on why that might be, but as she said to her eldest probably the truth would out eventually.

To say Peter was secretive about his private life would be unfair, because he tried very hard to be open, but years of working for the Police had worn off, and he was anything but. Dorothy had soon noticed something a bit Jeckyl and Hyde about him; whilst he could be thoughtful to a tee, he would on occasion insist that he was not to be corrected, when frankly one felt he must know he was in the wrong. This, with a sometimes obtruse and difficult manner left one wondering if he had any friends among his colleagues though perhaps he would have made a very good policeman, one couldn't say.

Certainly I think in the early days it had all been about chain of command or perhaps lack of it. Peter had a name for himself that he liked to see everything, every last scrap of detail, and although this was fine with his bosses, further down the ranks it brought frustration. As time went on, however, Peter was more able to pick and choose who he dealt with and he put together what was considered a formidable team.

Mrs. Finchley, had met what at first seemed a generous, well spoken, well educated young man with all the prospects one could possibly hope for; so what went wrong. Well he drank and when he drank he would drink to oblivion, and although there was nothing wrong in that in its self, more and more his wife began to worry for herself. She had spoken to her father and promised that on the first sign of violence she would leave him, not only that, but her father had insisted that once was enough and that it would be for good. With that in mind she had put having a family on hold.

Sure enough, and through no fault of her own, in a drunken stupor one evening he struck her, fearing for her life she made a bee line for the front door and escaped him. Pleading on the phone and promising that it would never happen again made no impression on her or her father and when a letter dropped through the letter box sueing for a divorce and possible annulment, finally Peter's head hung low and he felt the bitter sting of remorse, although at this time he still continued to drink.

Although she didn't say it obviously Dorothy was aware that something had gone wrong and though bear it she must, she could not understand how when her marriage had seemed better than ever her partner was taken from her. He had died so young surely that was unfair although she was forced to admit he hadn't really suffered, falling ill a month or two, no more, before the end. All these little revelations she shared with her eldest and the older he became the more she entrusted him with her opinions and views.

"I don't know why Peter's wife left him." She would say. "He seems a very kind man in many ways and he's ever so thoughtful. I think he'd do anything for you."
"Yes, I think he's very good in many ways." And with this Anthony gestured as if to take in all things.
"Of course I don't know how long he's been without a drink perhaps that has something to do with it. Though you must never say so. It's him, or her for that matter. Of course I don't really know what she was like, I think she just decided and off she went. More tea?"
"No thanks, I'm fine."

"Of course you know Mark has had his problems." This was not untypical of the way Dorothy often spoke throw away remarks that would unwittingly be the most important things she said.
"No."
"Yes, he came home and found the house empty thankfully I

think they have sorted the situation out, but he was a bit worried. Something to do with a misunderstanding with money I understand."

Somehow Mrs. Johnson was able to make a mountain more like a mole hill. Anthony sat thinking about what had just been said. He wondered if perhaps this was one of those instances where he should offer a little of himself. Somewhat gingerly he said.
"As you know I've had girlfriends but I've never really felt the urge to marry."
"Oh, you're all right," came the retort back, almost before Anthony had finished speaking.
"I just think you don't want to become too serious too quickly."
One sensed subject closed.
"Actually I often wonder what you would have done had you not become unwell." It was always unwell, rather than ill, somehow it sounded better. "Have you any idea what you would have liked to have done."
Unwittingly Anthony missed the point now was the time to compliment her by saying he would have enjoyed University but nothing was further from his mind and he answered, if not rather disappointingly, that he would have liked to have been a train driver. Anthony was a great lover of the railroad and while those that remembered steam thought that Diesel or Electric could never really match it for its romantic charm, the children of British Rail were in all probability as romantic about the post steam era as those that had come before them.
I don't like to think of Mrs. Johnson as a snob but in all truth she did not envisage her children doing manual labour and that she made known. Though in all truth it was perhaps as much through her fear as ignorance; that she imagined all such people to be illiterate and in a class with which frankly she had never had that much to do. Clearly Anthony in no way suffered from her prejudices and having worked in both the building trade and seen the factory floor, felt that in today's society that was unreasonable. Whilst Dorothy's opinions could not be changed she preferred to avoid the topic, although she would admit to her son that indeed things had changed enormously since her childhood and no there

was nothing wrong in that form of employ but had she been a man she wouldn't have chosen it. Her own husband had worked for a living as she saw it although he had gone from job to job.

"Anthony," she called. "Will you come and carve."
This was more of an assertion than a question and in Anthony's quiet manner he padded into the kitchen to help, as he would also with the dishes.

After the meal Mrs. Johnson put some tit bits on the lawn and in no time and to her obvious delight a big black bird swept down and took them. In all fairness and with Anthony's acquiescence I can inform the reader that in general Anthony was not a lover of animals but if he had a preference he liked the wild variety. I don't think there was any real reason for this although Anthony did frown on domesticated animals. One would love to report that perhaps he had been bitten by an animal when he was younger, but as far as he or anyone else could remember that wasn't so.

The afternoon passed quietly enough but again one felt that there was more significance in what hadn't been said, than there was in what had.

"Oh," she said. "Mrs. Maudley has died. I don't know whether you would have known her."
As a peeved expression crossed Anthony's face, he couldn't have been less interested had he tried, and why? What could this possibly have to do with him?
"Yes I have been invited to the funeral, though I don't know whether I will go to the Crematorium. There's bound to be a church service and I suppose there will be a reception at the house."
She paused.
"Mind you Mrs. Maudley was getting on a bit and as far as I know the only relative is her niece. I don't know what she'll do with the house, sell it I presume. Mind you I wouldn't mind knowing how much she will get for it."

Mrs. Maudley was not Mrs. Johnson's next door neighbour

Anthony Johnson

however as Mrs. Johnson would of put it she lived round the corner and had done so for as long as anyone could remember. Anthony would have loved to have asked who found her but having trod this ground before he didn't dare. He had only met her once, although he still remembered her. He had been taking some plums around from his mother's garden and she in turn had given him some beans, of the green variety, to take home with him. Even then she had seemed ancient and as well as knowing who found her he also wouldn't mind knowing just how old she was.

It wouldn't be unfair to say Anthony had a preoccupation with people's ages and whilst he had grown up believing that one shouldn't ask, at times he couldn't help himself. The most probable cause of this was his father's untimely early death.

Anthony's father, now there was a man where one almost had to draw a breath, and like many others Anthony was much in awe of the man. It was not that he held any great position but six foot four and with a character as congenial as anybody's people naturally migrated towards him. Having left the navy long after everyone else had been demobbed he had joined only a week or two before the war had ended, considering this could be a good career and a chance to see the world even after its war time ravages. He had, on the whole, enjoyed his years at sea. Returning to terra firma, partly for the love of Dorothy, and partly because he couldn't see himself as forever a sailor, he embarked on a number of projects; he found himself in sales, then as a manager, head of department, and then again in sales. The truth of it was that he was good with people and this meant he would be popular.

Dorothy, Dorothy Willard was her maiden name, had first met Derek Johnson when she had nursed him for malaria, like a lot of women just after the war she had felt she had a calling and that was nursing. Further to that she had suddenly found herself in the Royal Naval Hospital near Newark. Derek had arrived there presumably after an infection in the Tropics. He was taken very ill indeed.

Towards the end of Derek's stay in hospital Dorothy put it to him did he have someone to write to, he had been the black sheep of the family, and they had had difficulty contacting anyone that would serve as a next of kin. Without doubt the seeds of love had been sown and for the next two years Derek and Dorothy enjoyed a mounting stream of mail, further to this should Derek's ship dock at a British port be it Strathclyde or Portsmouth Dorothy was always there to meet him. The change was as evident in Derek as when he had first left home or gone to sea, and in Dorothy when she found herself nursing or first entering the Royal Navy. Reluctantly Derek was forced to admit that in all probability life with Dorothy was more important to him than sailing the seven seas and that and the understanding that he would be lucky to make petty officer he decided to leave. For herself Dorothy did not really see why their relationship should be exclusive of the Navy, but as Derek Johnson made his last journey the turning of his stomach was like that sickness which he had never felt.

Leaving the Naval Hospital to begin a family, Dorothy's life was one of marital bliss and similarly, neither she nor Anthony could truly accept the loss of the man they had known as Derek Johnson. The situation being further exacerbated by the swiftness of his demise and whilst some couples would find themselves on the brink of divorce, after ten years of marriage or more, Dorothy would have done anything she could to prolong their relationship. Smiling through the tears as she visited him for the last time he died quietly in his sleep.

Perhaps and as other families would have found it had it happened to them, Mark, Anthony and their mother could not believe the emotional void with which the death of their loved one left them. Conversely they had not bargained on the way in which it all seemed to bring them together. It is true to say that Anthony found the responsibilities of being the little man of the house on the one hand ingratiating and on the other a down right bloody nuisance. In Anthony's mind here he was accepting the responsibilities while barely out of shorts and although everyone praised him and said how mature he was, his mother was under no misgivings that he was still a child.

Anthony Johnson

As adolescence loomed and puberty began Anthony found himself lacking, not what you would have thought, those little chats one has with their parents, but the physical presence and truth that he felt when his father had been alive. But for all that life went on and relatively Mrs. Johnson found herself well off, they did not have to move house if they did not want to, nor would either of the two boys have to leave school. Mrs. Johnson while not really going without anything had always watched the pennies, but now it became clear that really there had and indeed still was plenty of money around.

It was funny that, that she had known her husband had had a fairly good job, they lived in a nice house, they had always had a family holiday, there seemed to be a nice car parked in the drive, but somehow Dorothy just had not seemed to notice. It wasn't that she was ungrateful, far from it; it was almost as if Derek had protected her from it; now she had to do the books herself she could neither believe there was so much to spend or the relative costs of things she was likely to spend it upon. The truth of just how able Derek had been with money only seemed to come out now.

Had Anthony inherited his father's monetary ability I think in the economic climate of the day he would have soon found himself a millionaire, however he rejected his father's attitude towards politics and wealth and certainly in his twenties was little more than a closet socialist. His mother became increasingly tired of this and up until the time when he had fallen ill frequently badgered him about it. Why would a well educated boy like him want to work on a building site or in a packing factory? And wasn't it typical of the socialists they were socialists because they could afford to be. Anthony would not be drawn on this replying that the other option was one of greed and lined no others than those in power's pockets and that he did not hold with material gain as an objective in itself. It was exactly this kind of idealism that made going to university seem like a good idea, not only to broaden ones own horizons, but a chance to enjoy the political debate through the students union.

So why had he dropped out? Or perhaps why did he decide

to do something else? Sure enough he went through all the rigmarole of filling in U.C.C.A. application forms and attended several interviews but despite the quite reasonable grades he achieved, he felt like a fish out of water as he spoke to students who were already attending. He couldn't help it, he felt terribly inadequate. Attending one interview he arrived in London several hours before he need be and had gone into a pub where for an hour he knocked back the scotch, this University College would not be offering him a place. Finally he was able to achieve the middle ground as he saw it; he would take a year out from his studies but would confirm that he had a place for the following year, at last everyone would be satisfied.

Mark, following in his footsteps did not make the same mistake; for whilst Anthony was taking his year out he discovered on the one hand there was such a thing as money and on the other there was such a thing as sex. The money would have been enough in itself, he was taking home three times as much as his mother could expect to earn from nursing and going against the moral and religious code of his parent he could see nothing wrong with just moving in with someone. Looking back on his life he would wonder what would have happened had he married the girl, for secretly he had known from living together for just a week or two that would have been a disaster. Emily, Anthony's first real partner was frankly pathetic. At the time however he had been in love with her but for all that she was completely unable to do anything for herself. When things came to an end one knew it would be a wrench, Anthony kept it to himself just how much he had loved her and how glad he was it had ended.

During the whole nightmare, as Dorothy saw it, she had refused to contact him; he could contact her but she would make no attempt unless it came from him first. Later Dorothy would wonder whether had Anthony not met Emily he would have kept his promise to go to University or perhaps would have settled down to some kind of married life. She would not cry over spilt milk but sometimes she thought to herself perhaps that was just the way her son was. Anthony for his part held secret misgivings about his sixth form education and said if he could have had his time again he would probably have gone into the services. This may sound strange coming from our little left winger but Anthony had another side to his character and it was that that he felt would have been satisfied had he entered the army. Starting young Anthony had built quite a collection of things military, he liked anything from a horse's bridle from the battle of Waterloo to a picture or a model of the latest fighter plane. As quite a young man he would approach soldiers or pilots when the army were recruiting but to follow in his father's footsteps that he couldn't for although he did not like to admit it he was afraid of the sea.

Funnily enough Anthony was not frightened of water, he could wash shave and bathe in it, and in a somewhat half hearted attempt to deny his fears he had also been to a swimming baths. But he could remember it like yesterday, how he had stood on the beach watching the waves crashing into the shore, terrorized. You see it was not that it was wet that frightened him it was the sheer size, mass, depth and distance that crippled him. He could no more think of taking a plane over the ocean than a boat the distance between him and land was impossible to contemplate. Given these misgivings one wonders how he would have ever gone abroad but in his late teens he had flown to Paris and from that trip on he had the bug although he insisted on flying rather than brave the elements on board a ferry.

Emily and Anthony lived together for the best part of two years. I cannot begin to explain the relief Anthony felt on having his first relationship under his belt. Before Emily there had not really been anyone, he felt that probably his associates at college felt he tried too hard, this may have been true, but then if he was not to try, how would he ever meet anyone anyway. Anthony was unable to rationalise this situation and for the bulk of his latter years in school he lived on friends successes rather than his own. How strange it was then when on that day in late September, early October, he walked in to a bar and on the flimsiest pretexts introduced himself to Emily.

Sitting at the bar she was talking to a friend.

"Oh you are from the north," he ventured. It was fairly obvious that she was since she had the accent.
"Which side, Lancashire or Yorkshire." Realising what a stupid thing he had just said he blushed. That was like asking a Scotsman if he came from Ireland. She took it well and almost laughed.
"We're not all from Barnsley," she said making the accent even stronger.
"Do you want a drink?" It then dawned that she was drinking with some friends, quite how it happened Anthony was never quite sure but they invited him to join them. Not to be unfair Anthony was not really interested in her friends, they seemed dishevelled, rough, rugged folk, and Anthony was all too aware how he might be taken as an inverted snob, although he was forced to admit these were not the sort of people with whom he had ever had much to do.

Eventually a table became available and the two of them left the others who carried on drinking steadily at the bar. Emily for her part was interested in this rather incongruous, rather fool hardy man who was not afraid to step on others toes, but as luck would have it she was not seeing anyone at the moment, although that was not something that ever worried her anyway.

There she sat opposite him, ringlet curls, a pretty rounded face, and a voluptuous body that was all curves and wonton flesh. Before the evening was half way through Anthony was at her for a second date, he didn't dare to tell her that he was living at home, so that when she asked where she could contact him all he could think of doing was offering her his work number; all right the lads on site would rag him blind if she called, but that would be infinitely better than his mother passing remarks over the dinner table. Anthony did not really even care to let his brother know what was happening, and when Anthony finally plucked up courage to tell them about his girl and that he was thinking of leaving home, his brother himself was only months away from his first date. Where as Anthony had left school really without a friend or ally to speak of, his brother did exactly the opposite and went on to be a member of the old boys football and rugby clubs, always the life and soul of the party our Mark.

Anthony Johnson

So it was that on the Tuesday after that weekend a call came through to the site managers office where Anthony was working shuffling round bits of paper and generally making a nuisance of himself.
"Emily," his voice went all soft and silky.
"Yes.... Yes.... Yes." He held his hand over the mouth piece and whispered to one of the other fellows that it was his girl friend.
"Well don't mind me," the bloke said.
"Yes... Yes... Oh, all right then. Yes see you then." And with that he rang off.
"Going to the pictures tonight," ventured Anthony.
"You won't be going bloody anywhere unless you get this mess sorted out. Now where's this invoice."
Anxious and ecstatic the afternoon could not have gone any more slowly had the clock stopped altogether. As he had done ever since he was in the sixth form he cycled home, he would get in, wash maybe even shave, sit down to his tea and then be gone again.
"I hope she's worth it," his mother would call after him.

He arrived at the pictures a good half an hour early and became more and more agitated as time went by. He couldn't bare to think about it but then he couldn't think of anything else. What would he do if she didn't turn up, but with seconds rather than minutes round the corner she came.
"You cut it a bit close."
"I am sorry," she said and kissed him on the cheek. No further explanation was given. Anthony fidgeted all through the film, the weather was warm and the air stifling in the cinema. The seats were sticky and Anthony could feel the sweat run down his back. They held hands a bit but neither of them could really get comfortable. At last the house lights went on and the picture was over. Anthony hadn't a clue what he had been watching and frankly he did not care.

Desperate to know whether Emily would invite him in or say goodbye on the doorstep Anthony hardly said a word as they walked home. Emily knew by now that Anthony was living at home and although it was not her consideration it was however Anthony's; what would his mother say if he was to stay out all night. As it turned out Anthony's fears were allayed; he would at least sleep in his own bed which left his mother asking no more than what time he had come in, and for this Anthony could tell a little white lie.

The following week however he told his mother that he would be spending the night at a friends house and this situation would have continued but for Emily and he deciding that they would shack up together. Dorothy was not really a narrow minded person although one couldn't help feeling that her values were from a by gone age. She had no real objection to Anthony having a girlfriend but when it went as far as living together, there she felt the line should be drawn. It was not the sex or living together that annoyed her, she felt had Emily been any decent girl she would have wanted to marry and Anthony, well somehow she did not see him in quite the same light. He after all had all the advantages of a sexual relationship and none of the deadly ties that could spoil a marriage. Further, Anthony's mum could see that he was almost light headed with love.

As soon as Anthony moved in there were problems, Emily only did a couple of hours work a day, and Anthony soon found she was often strapped for cash. This and other things such as her complete inability to do anything in the kitchen, which meant she either relied on Anthony to take her out or as was becoming more and more the case he would come in after a full days work and then cook. He wondered what she had done before they had met. Bottom line he felt she had probably gone without. I draw these conclusions in a manner that Anthony perhaps would have done more recently for at the time he was besotted, he was in love and he couldn't get enough of her. Every day he would turn up for work looking more and more tired, the men passed remarks under his nose but he didn't notice or perhaps he didn't care.

At the weekend he would just crash like the proverbial computer. He would lie in bed until gone midday and then getting washed and dressed nearer to tea time than lunch he began drinking. For some years albeit that he was under age Anthony had been able to get served and although he'd never been a big drinker this was beginning to change. At Emily's he didn't have the drinks cabinet that his mother had kept or the small sherry glasses nor was he only drinking beer anymore - he could quite happily finish off the best part of a bottle of scotch before Sunday. At that age he was not concerned about alcoholism nor did anyone think it was anymore than high jinks.

Life went on at Dorothy's in spite of her losing her first son, Mark was hot on his heels and made it obvious that he would start dating long before his brother had. Anthony, now able to shrug off the responsibilities that had for so long controlled and constricted his life, however felt the need to keep in touch and after he had let Dorothy down on a couple of appointments that he had made, she began to become increasingly worried about him. But her mind was made up unless it came from Anthony she would have no contact with her son.

After a number of months when Anthony had burnt the candle at both ends and regularly drank to oblivion, he was brought down to earth with a bump. He lost his job. Thankfully he had been saving carefully and that would break the fall, but gone were the plans to buy a car and or have a holiday abroad. When Dorothy heard of this she almost breathed a sigh of relief perhaps now he would give up this female and return to his studies. But nothing could have been further from Anthony's thoughts. For a while Anthony would claim the welfare but he became increasingly erratic, he would go out and spend their money then draw on his bank account. Ideologically he seemed unsound declaring that those who did not want to work shouldn't on the grounds that there was only so much work to go around, hence he continued claiming. Emily did not really like having Anthony out of work and as he blazed ahead saying it would give that much more time for them to be together she quietly fumed. Emily, refusing to believe that her life was an easy ticket, felt more and more contempt for the young Anthony. Okay he did more than his share of household duties and was more able to cook than her, he was not in her opinion a manly man. From his point of view he couldn't win; if he left her the chores and suggested she cook it generally turned out a disaster, and although he couldn't see it she was incredibly lazy.

When he began spending more of his day at home he soon realised just how shallow her day was. She would go to the creche to do her two hours first thing in the morning, that meant about ten o'clock. She came home and spent most of the rest of the day stuck in front of the T.V. she would watch practically anything. One day Anthony was just coming in having been to the library she was watching children's T.V. He didn't know how it happened he just came out with it, did she want a baby, she got up and went into the bedroom and as he was stood in the doorway she sat on the bed screaming and beating her pillow, in floods of tears. He never broached the subject again. For his part he had been sure she would welcome him spending more time at home but it was not so. Towards the end of his unenforced period of unemployment he wrote to his mother, when there was no one else he could at least turn to her. Initially he had sat down with no intention of sending the letter - he just wanted to clear the air but in the end he sent it anyway.

When Dorothy received this letter she knew immediately it was from her son and with a sense of gloom and despondency she opened it and looked at the hand writing and layout before reading it through. This marked some sort of change - before he had only rung. It admitted that he had found it hard being out of work but not as he had expected her to think because of money, he made some attempt to beef up the relationship with Emily. He said he had toyed with becoming a vegetarian, that hurt far more that he could have known it would and finally he drew reference to his drinking. Almost immediately Dorothy began to draft a reply, but it was in her mind alone, she would not respond.

Eventually Anthony managed to find himself another job. This time he was working as a clerk in a bottling factory dealing with the audit. He had managed to convince someone at the job centre that he was the man for the job having worked in invoicing at the site. He was again struck with a sense of inadequacy, it was not him it was the job, he was only there for the money, but wasn't everyone, he couldn't imagine this to be the sort of work for which one had a calling. Anthony being away from home and his brother safely into the sixth form, Mrs. Johnson spent more time working than she had done in recent years. For her nursing was a calling, because Anthony, in the money again, wanted to make a small sum over to her; he was quite surprised when she agreed without question, and wondered whether he should have done so earlier. Anthony still hadn't his car nor had he had his foreign holiday but he felt quietly relieved and for a while he almost began behaving like a mature adult.

A year had passed and Anthony had the dubious chore of writing to the university that had offered him a place. Rightly or wrongly he assumed they would not delay his attendance for another year and so he had to reluctantly inform them that he would not be attending. This would make his mother fume but Emily gave him the nod, she might be the only one but she felt sure it was for the best. With that out of the way he began thinking about what he was going to spend his life doing, did he want to be a salesman, a rep, he could sort of envisage driving round the countryside making small deliveries and suggesting such and such's store would do better to sell this brand than that.

He thought about his father, how he had always kept money matters away from the rest of the family, he would try and do that for Emily. His relationship with her had flourished since he had returned to work and he was drinking far less and sleeping better at night. He did not want to know what she spent the day doing - all he cared about was that she should be affectionate and available to him and Emily herself rallied a little to the cause. She was more demonstrative and looked forward to his home comings each evening.

When the university with whom Anthony was planning to study wrote back to inform him that he no longer had a place, it was an anonymous typed letter of no more than a couple of lines. Anthony had written not really thinking there would be any definite reply, however he was stunned. It was so formal he could almost feel the ground open beneath him. He was not under the protectorate of his mother or his college he would not now be going to university, he would not be going into the services, suddenly his whole life flashed before him, what was he going to do.

As can happen in relationships he had imagined at the out set that this was a match that would surely last. However with the passing of time he had at first began living from month to month then it was from week to week then day to day, surely something must break. He was drinking in earnest again. It was at this point that Mrs. Johnson did something at present hitherto unimaginable, it was around lunch time and her shift did not begin for another couple of hours. She went to Anthony's street and just stood outside his flat. She was not a bit afraid, and for no other reason than the fact that it was there to do she looked in his dustbin, what she saw frankly shocked her there was bottle after bottle of spirits. Still she would not contact her son.

Although Mark was there and at an age that had it been Anthony Dorothy probably would have confided in him, she did not. Quite aware that Mark was quickly reaching manhood and would soon start bringing girls home, she would have felt uneasy and embarrassed at discussing Anthony's problems with him. Neither would she discuss it with Peter, but if there was anyone in whom she would confide it was their G.P. He however was unwilling to preside over any witch hunt and whilst he sympathised with both Dorothy and Anthony he could do little more than offer to mediate, and since Anthony was unwilliing in that, he really felt his hands tied. One would have thought that Dorothy could have spoken to Emily first hand but she did not, bit by bit she became less worried about their relationship continuing and more concerned on the affect it would have on Anthony should it end.

It was early one Sunday morning in June. Anthony should have been packing his bags to return home from university, instead he washed and dressed albeit casually, had a couple of cups of coffee and set off to attend the family service at one of the larger churches in the area. Frankly Anthony, however intrusive to his private life it would have been, would have liked a fire and brimstone sermon, but making reference to the love of God and Jesus, one couldn't help but feel that this was not to be the miraculous rebirth of Christian belief in the neighbourhood. Then there were the messages this person and his newly wedded wife had been short listed among others to carry out missionary activities in Kwala Lumpa. There was a blessing and some of the congregation took the communion, Anthony stayed in his seat.

Anthony would have loved to have been able to go up to the vicar and ask him if he could take him into his confidence, almost as he imagined a confessional would have been. Instead he shook his hand leaving the church and tried to put his problems to the back of his mind. Whilst I am sure the vicar would have coped well enough should he have been asked, it was not untypical of Anthony to show signs of fear dealing with figures of authority. He would have loved to have gone away and wept, but although he was deeply unhappy he knew he could shed no tears. One almost despairs at the irony of this situation for unknown to him Emily did weep. She wept after he had left the house in the morning, she wept on her own in the afternoon. She did not weep in front of Anthony, and the more she wept the more she felt used, used as a sexual play thing, used to keep Anthony from his mother's criticism, used by Anthony to shield him from his poor work record.

When she finally made the break she could not believe the relief she felt, their relationship had been claustrophobic in extreme. For more than a month she had wondered how she would make the break, in the end she had to break it to him.

Anthony also knew it was over, though he himself was more reluctant to admit it than her. When she told him that she was going to spend a couple of weeks at her mother's in the North he knew she would not be coming back, he could wait in vain for a letter but he knew in all probability that was unlikely. For the first time in nearly two years he decided to invite himself over to his mother's, he could say in all confidence that his relationship with Emily was over.

On his arrival at the family home, his home coming was not

greeted with relief, love and affection, in fact his mother took the attitude it was good of him to visit at all, seeing that he was his own boss and everything. Anthony couldn't believe it - no sooner had one door opened than another had slammed shut. Having showed him how she felt she had been treated she moved onto another bone of contention - his drinking. Anthony was naturally guarded about this, and would say no more than he had at times a lot to drink but did not reckon for him at least it was the road to ruin that surely his mother felt it was.

He left after an hour or so feeling that he'd been given a bit of an ear bashing, he didn't want to go back to the flat and the thought of going to the boozer filled him with trepidation, so for a while he just walked about. Some how as if the Holy Spirit had guided him he found himself outside the church, it wasn't locked so he went in and sat at the back. Looking down towards the altar, he did not know what to think had the Holy Spirit shined kindly upon him, it was not the sort of question that was easily asked.

Unnoticed by Anthony as he entered the church and two or three pews to his rear and a little to his right sat Lucinda Draycot, known to her friends as Lucy. She was still wearing the nurses uniform that she wore to work; her shift had finished just after lunch. She had shoulder length blonde hair which she wore up held with a clasp and her figure, whilst on the small side, was not yet petite. The uniform, which didn't really fit any of the nurses, had been altered but still erred on the ungainly side. Lucy sat looking down the nave at the altar and its enormous crucifix her hands lay placidly in her lap. She saw Anthony walk the small distance down the aisle to take up a place in front of her. He knelt and said a prayer then he too sat and looked up at the crucifix. He didn't say anything, he didn't need to; Lucy could see the desperation in him and her heart went out to him. Tucked inside one of the prayer books was an invitation to a youth fellowship meeting that took place every other Sunday. Anthony made a mental note to attend after evening prayers were said. Make no mistake about it Anthony was no more than a part time Christian and at times his agnosticism bordered on atheism. However he bitterly felt the need to be involved in something as one of the girls from work had said you don't want to let yourself be monopolized, he didn't have the heart to tell her that that was exactly what had happened. Although he was bitterly upset about the failure of his relationship with Emily, it was his fault and his alone that there was seemingly no one to whom he could turn.

Sure enough the evening of the youth fellowship meeting came around and Anthony spruced himself up a bit, he felt first impressions were important. The evening service finished just after seven and the youth fellowship evening was about to start a few minutes later in the crypt. Anthony noticed that in the crypt there was a tea and coffee bar and taking a cup he joined a group that had formed at the end of the room.

"Firstly and as I expect you can see, as I can, we have two new members who have joined our group and so as not to embarrass them if we could all go round and say our names."
"So I particularly want to thank Anthony and Lucy for having joined us here, and perhaps we could all say a prayer."

Much of the rest of that evening went by without stopping. Anthony found this group of young Christian's devotionals not just embarrassing but bordering on the absurd. He did not thank God for guiding him to this little group he had found his own way here, he didn't have to shout, "Lord be praised," after every remark that was made in the Lord's name. After about an hour and a half the group broke to take tea and coffee, if it had been a bar he would have asked for a strong one. He stood in one corner of the crypt absolutely wooden as a people circulated trying to say kind Christian things to one another.

Lucy also stood with her back to a wall, like Anthony, she didn't really hold with what was going on here. However when pressed Anthony fudged it he said the evening had been interesting if nothing else, he couldn't say whether he would come again but he felt honour bound to thank them all the same. Lucy made it quite clear that she was not into evangelical Christianity and though the group member who had addressed her was at pains to point out that wasn't the emphasis, she very nearly asked for her coat. Later Anthony wondered that had she left would they have been asked to pray for her return. Neither of them felt that their Christian views were best served by this scheme, neither of them felt they were particularly sinful, or that necessarily God's love would pass them by. This for all the world could have been the last time they ever met but it wasn't.

Anthony for his part had found that she often went to sit in the church after a shift and if he was careful and did not over do it he could meet her there from time to time. Lucinda on her part had found out that Anthony's mother and her shared a career.

So it was then that when Anthony's twenty first birthday came around it was Lucy that Mrs. Johnson turned to for inspiration. In the end it was something so exciting that she bought she could hardly contain herself. It was a metal detector. The logic behind this was what with Anthony's interest in things military he could go to various sites and prospect, who knows what he might find. At first he was a bit uneasy about it, he didn't know when he'd use it, but as he held it as one would and put on the ear piece, it grew on him, in fact it grew and grew.

Lucy for her part gave Anthony a wallet and would have loved to have made some sort of a quip about him keeping it near to his heart. There was no doubt about it; in the last few months Anthony's quality of life had dramatically improved. He had loved Emily and to himself at least he admitted it but things had been so chaotic, one never had time to look over one's shoulder before the next onslaught began. Lucy somehow had breathed an air of stability, the air was fresh but consistent.
"I'm working a late on Saturday, but you could still come over."
Anthony was only too ready to accept this invitation, although he had a thing about women who attended church - wrongly or rightly he imagined they wouldn't do anything without at least the offer of a ring. She had said about quarter to nine and if he was very lucky she might cook. He

didn't know whether anyone else had been invited consequently he wasn't quite sure what to wear. He sat in the bath and decided that wearing a suit was going a bit too far, though he would wear a jacket and trousers that way if they went to a club he'd still be allowed in.

Anthony would have loved to tell Lucy that he was on the rebound, that sounded so adult. He didn't however for fear of spoiling his chances. He arrived sweet smelling and anything if not but nervous. He went up the steps and rang the bell. Lucy came down, she was still wearing her uniform. "Oh you look smart." She said. "You must excuse me I've only been home a few minutes and I've had to put the cooking going."
They were going to eat, that was a relief. As he went up the stairs to her little flat he could sense it, nay smell it; this was bedsit land where corridors smelt of cabbage, joss-sticks and stale sheets. After the stair well her own part of the house was atypical. The walls were clean maybe even recently painted, bright yellows and oranges. The furniture was old but it had been looked after, and one could imagine that Lucy was probably on quite good terms with her landlord. The smaller of the two rooms she had, served as a kitchen diner, the other as a bedroom sitting room. One couldn't tell immediately whether she had lived here a long time or a matter of months. All of a sudden it hit Anthony just how little he knew about her, about anyone. Why did she attend church after her shift? He had wondered whether it was grief was she praying for a patient that had died a terrible death, or had she done something, he didn't know what.

"Smells nice."
"Yes," she said. "It's a vegetable curry. We can eat when you like. Just say the word. No need to stand on formalities in my house."
"I know you like a drink so I got a bottle in, but promise me you won't finish it tonight. Or you won't be invited again." With that she smiled broadly.
"With that in mind," said Anthony. "I wouldn't mind a cup of tea."
"To that you are always welcome." She smiled again.

Anthony went through to the lounge area and immediately became embroiled in her book shelf.
"You can put some music on if you want to? I don't know what you like. I'll be through in a minute.
In fact Anthony carried on looking through the book collection and when Lucy came in he said just one word, "philately."
"Yes I admit it. I can't help it. But you are a collector too, or so I've heard."
"Yes but in comparison with this I might as well collect nick nacks."
"You're too modest."
"And discs are you a collector to those too."
"Well I know what I like, and I like what I know."
Sitting down in an armchair Anthony was still browsing a book of stamps from the occupation of France and wondering how they ever got delivered. Over in the corner of the room was a radiogram, a sort of record player come radio which all in the same cabinet had speakers as well. Again very collectable.

"If you'll excuse me I think I ought to change. Oh and leave the door it'll let some air in."

Anthony went out to the kitchen.
"There is a bag with some booze in it, by the side of the cooker. Help yourself."
As Anthony turned round with the bag he realised he could see Lucy through the door and in her wardrobe mirror. Immediately he wondered whether she could see him, well if she could she wasn't making it plain. There she stood. She had taken off her uniform and was admiring herself on tip toes. She held her bosom in her hands almost as if she was weighing them. Then she walked smartly over to her wardrobe and took out a short black dress. Anthony wouldn't have missed it for the world. She brushed her hair and came into the kitchen.
"You couldn't do me up could you? she asked. Was Anthony mistaken or as he fixed her fastener did she press her body into his.
"Did you watch?" she asked.

Anthony Johnson

"Well no, or maybe just a little," Anthony replied.
"I don't mind I'm proud of my body," and then completely changing the subject she said, "Would you like to see my party trick?"
Feeling less embarrassed now, Anthony said he would. She took his hand and led him into the other room. "There you are sit in the arm chair," and without any further notice she went down to the floor in the splits. If Anthony felt impressed at this, what was to follow would seem almost bizarre. Coming up from the splits and then sitting down again crossed legged, she proceeded to put her foot first up to her mouth and then behind her head. Once again sitting cross legged she smiled broadly and said, "Do you want me?"
He did.

The next day or in fact the same day because Anthony hadn't left until the early hours, Lucy phoned him to ask if he would like to go out in her car and possibly bring the metal detector. Initially his new toy would be as interesting to her as to him. So they decided to take the car to Gosport the scene of one of the civil war battles. It is true the sun wasn't shining but it looked as if the rain would hold off. After the steamy evening they had had last night both of them felt they could use some fresh air. As Lucy pulled up outside Anthony's flat Anthony was already ready. He embraced her and then became very matter of fact about putting things into the car. He was obviously a bit tetchy.

She drove one of those VW Beetles and it was only by raising ones voice that one could make ones self heard over the noise of the engine. They didn't speak that much. It was only a half hours drive. Lucy had brought a thermos flask and decided to sit in the car and have a cuppa. She had also brought a book. Anthony donned the headphones and set across the field with his metal detector. I think initially he had imagined himself covering a huge area with the odd precious find here and there. It came as a surprise then that every few paces his metal detector stopped him and he had to do a little digging to see what he had found. About half way through the afternoon he also stopped for a cup of coffee. He had a small bag of things he had found, Lucy was delighted, he had everything from an old coke tin to a belt buckle, from and arrow head to a ball bearing. Surprising perhaps but he also had money. She was pleased for him. Strickly speaking what he had found should have been declared treasure trove. But as Anthony was no way sure he was going to keep up the hobby he didn't bother.

"I'm some what perplexed by you," Lucy said. "You have obviously had a good education, you are well spoken and intelligent, yet you are working in a dead end factory. Almost as if you didn't care. And I say this to you because I do. Care I mean."
Not a man used to much criticism Anthony took this on the chin. Had Emily ever said that to him he would have gone into a rage, but somehow from Lucy he could take it.

"Well when I left school I had to look for work. I needed the money. The first job I had was working on a site."
"A building site?"
"Yes. But then I mucked them about and I left......."
"But didn't it occur to you to go to university."
"Well it did, but when the time came."
"You see it strikes me that a man like you should not really be working in a factory."
"At the risk of seeming crude would it be that different if I worked in a Bank."

The subject was closed.

It was about this time that Anthony met David. David was obviously a public schoolboy with a plum in his mouth to prove it. He was also a graduate though no one seemed to know quite in what. Surprising then that he had ended up working on the shop floor next to Anthony. The two of them immediately took a liking for one another and I think it was Anthony that suggested they go out for a pint. David was just the tonic Anthony was dying for. Did David view life through the same socialist tinted spectacles as Anthony? Well in fact no, but all the same there was plenty to discuss and argue about. Anthony would sit enthralled listening to tales of David's undergraduate days. David had only really come into the factory when he couldn't find anything else, he was still looking for permanent employ, though he was forced to admit the wages were by no means detrimental to his burdening bank balance. David, not unlike Lucy, was someone Anthony could feel he could readily introduce to his mother.

She would congratulate him on his masters and say that she had hoped that Anthony would go on to further education. She would say how she felt Anthony was quite bright enough and tell of how well he had done at school. Then there was Mark now he also looked as if he was going to university. Lucy would speak in soft tones to her, proud that she was a fellow nurse. Peter, who had left the police force, always seemed slightly surprised to see him when he did.

As time progressed Lucy challenged Anthony more and more, she wanted him to do something, anything but to use his time constructively and the more Anthony denied her criticism the further he was thrown into despondency. He hated to admit it but he was chronically bored and disinterested in his work. But for all that he had managed to put some money behind him and was in fact looking forward to the day when he would no longer work there.

I don't think Lucy was aware of just how much of a hold she had over Anthony. He was at a point where had it been feasible he probably would have asked her to marry him. Yet it was not. She had stated categorically that she would not marry him or live in sin, but if he could accept these premises she would be happy to have a relationship with him. It turned out that she had in fact been married, having wedded in the very beginning of her twenties; suffice it to say it had been a complete disaster. It was for his soul as well as for her own that she prayed in the church "Deliver us from evil" it sounded so apt.

She did believe that God's only son had died on the cross so that our sins might be forgiven. She did believe that through the power of prayer we may be redeemed.

Was she beginning to sound like one of those Christians that met after church, had these thoughts been anything other than private that might have been true but they were not. I think both Anthony and Lucy benefited from that fact that they were not living one upon the other and certainly Anthony liked the idea that he was not bound to her and could go out with David with impunity. From time to time the three of them would go out together and if it was required Lucy would drive allowing the other two to please themselves what they drank. She looked on as the two of them, quite oblivious to the world, would philosophize about man's great dilemma through a drunken haze. She may have felt that she could see a little more how her friends were than they may have of her, but at the end of the day she was glad to have two such loyal friends.

David for his part did well to hide the resentment that he felt towards Anthony. He didn't like to speak of it but his days at university had not really gone that well at all. To make up for this he made up a lot of what he had to say: drunken parties late into the night, women falling over one another. He did not know it but secretly Lucy had her apprehensions, and as the tales became taller and taller Anthony also took him less and less seriously. But that is how it is with such people, they can change tack and deny all that they've said at the drop of a hat only to start a new story with as much substance as the first.

Some people would have found that intolerable in a man but Lucy and Anthony found it curiously entertaining, they loved to play along whether the story went on to have its substance in truth or not. Sometimes the three of them would be joined by a fourth, a girl called Angie who also worked at the packing factory. This led to a little intrigue whether Angie and David were an item or whether he had just asked her to make up the four. Anthony had often watched her working as he had other girls working on the factory floor. It may sound unlikely but it was true that almost all the women that worked at the packing factory were either young or much older, there didn't seem to be any middle ground. Anthony assumed this was because women in their late twenties and early thirties went home to have their children. Thus Angie was in her twenties but again not at all what you would expect. She didn't mind working there at all, in fact she would admit that she quite liked it. The work was repetitious but that was O.K. you didn't really have to concentrate on what you were doing - it came as second nature and there were breaks and one could talk to the other girls. Then there was over time and one could opt to change a duty if one was unhappy at it. Yes it wasn't a bad job. The only thing they really cared about was being on time.

This was something Lucy would reflect upon; she could quite understand how punctuality could be so important. She shared with Angie the feeling that she worked as part of a team. The two men however both held their work in some contempt and felt little or no loyalty to the packing factory. As I have said both of them were looking forward to a time when they would no longer work there. It had been suggested, by whom I don't know, that seeing as David had a degree that perhaps he could go into teaching, though frankly the very thought of it left him cold. For him as much as for Anthony he felt that the important thing was to be earning some money and whilst his expenses at University had not been enormous he still had that little matter of an overdraft to consider. Anthony had begun to wonder whether he would save up a sum and then perhaps put himself through college but somehow any concrete ideas about what he should study or where still alluded him. Lucy for her part had wondered about Anthony's interest in Art and although she could no more see him as an artist than say David or anyone else for that matter, she felt perhaps a leaning towards the fine arts would be no bad thing, and with that in mind she felt curiously reassured.

Lucy approached Dorothy, Anthony's mother, and all though at first she drew a complete blank the very thought that perhaps Anthony was beginning once again to consider his options delighted Mrs. Johnson. Although at first they would speak over the phone, admittedly at some length, later Lucy would be invited to the family home, it was then that they would speak at length, and among other things the matter of the metal detector had been discussed. Mrs. Johnson was quite adamant about it she would do anything she could to further her boys career, that is assuming he was to have a career. For her part Lucy explained how she had met

Anthony at the church and indeed at the time how he had seemed very down. Mrs. Johnson bit her lip and said nothing of her boy's previous relationship. She didn't know how much Anthony had said and as the better side of judgement she decided to stay out of it. Lucy also told her a bit about her former partner and how after only a couple of months it, had been obvious that their marriage had gone past the point of no return. This was inconceivable to Mrs. Johnson, how could they have been married if it was all over so soon, again she kept her thoughts on the matter to herself.

When the two of them parted in the latter half of that afternoon they did so amicably. But Anthony would later recall how his mother expressed her fears of the two of them getting too intimate long after they had happily fulfilled each others needs. So it remained a secret that Anthony and Lucy shared and as they were not really living together they both felt that the details of their intimacy were best kept private.

To say Anthony and David were best friends is almost to undermine a relationship that seemed unmoveable. There was a bond between them that bordered on a family tie. One was indebted as the other or so at first it seemed. David had been the only son of a Doctor, however he was not a G.P. but a surgeon. As much as David may have liked it or not he was expected to follow in father's footsteps. This was fine until he fluncked his exams and was forced to wait to see whether he had a place at university at all. He had, but in History, which enraged his father even more; what practical use had a degree in history. But as David knew a degree was a degree and just that in its self opened doors. There were all sorts of practical use, one could find oneself working in a bank or any fairly large sized firm where management postions may be open to him; or perhaps in advertising, or for that matter with the B.B.C. or other broad casting organisation. The one thing he was was optimistic and although, not unlike his school days, his university studies were somewhat lack lustre, he left college with a certain zest for life.

As we know David had gone into the packing factory almost as one did in the holidays, although he would not now be returning to university. Behind his back the girls loved to make fun of him, they would call him Lord Jim, and mouthed the way he pronounced his words. They were not to know that he was aware of what they were doing and so it might be called brave that he asked Angie to join him for a drink. The week following his date the girls were almost riotous as they fired questions at Angie. For example, did he ask you what colour your knickers were, and, I bet you couldn't wait to tell him. Through all this Angie covered her face with her hands, blushing brightly, while the others shrieked with laughter.

One of the older women passed David on the gantry where the offices were.
"Take no notice, love. They're only jealous."
David enjoyed all the fuss and couldn't wait to take her out again; maybe it would excite her even more; though he had to admit that in many ways one was as good as another.

It must be said that while the middle classes, which most probably included David as much as Anthony, were suffering some form of moral breakdown, it was apparent that these factory girls were in every respect completely opposite. They did not have sex before marriage, their mothers probably terrifying them with the threat of sexual diseases and distrust over any man that said he would use a condom.

Their social and moral outlook may have been out of the Ark but for all that Anthony couldn't help but admire their outspoken joy and gaiety and their light hearted playfulness. They were what they were - working girls.

Anthony hadn't thought to mention it but as David also found almost all of the girls that worked there had known each other long before they had gone there to work. In fact for many of them they not only worked there but the mother's had also, a handful of whom had now returned to work.

After about six weeks of David dating Angie he suddenly found himself called into the office. The boss wanted to see him, though as David was forced to admit he didn't know why. As it turned out the chief said that he had been following the (how shall we call them) developments between Angie and him, and although he wouldn't have usually seen it as his place to intervene, well frankly it wasn't but he felt David should at least be made to understand that before it went too far what he was letting himself in for. Eventually the penny dropped and David said more than intimacy, "much more." It occurred to David that she might expect to marry, that was it. Thanking the boss he left his office only to run headlong into an older woman that he had also got to know.

Her first words were "take no notice, he thinks he's god almighty sat up in that office all day, mark my words Angie would love a bit of loving, and going around with your crowd, what's she to lose at your age."

David paced off to his station shaking his head, women, men, the boss, who needed them. He was going to need that pint tonight perhaps then he and Anthony could talk things over. As best laid plans are never kept, in fact Anthony was going over to Lucy's and the two of them would not need any other company. David understood they had been going out a lot and hadn't had that much time for each other, secretly he fumed. David went home to his little bed sitting studio flat even now he could not express his anger, so it was that he sat there playing patience with a deck of cards. Tired and irritable that he was, his mind ranged over the women he knew, the girls working at the factory, people he had passed in the street. But in there somewhere Lucy was reprimanding him. Why was that so? Did he like to feel he had put one over on Anthony? No not really. How did he feel about Anthony? They were best mates were they not? Yes well in that case he was bound to understand. There, he sat late into the night, playing with the cards until eventually his eyes would feel so heavy he was forced to turn in.

The next day Anthony seemed reluctant to talk about his evening and because of this I think David automatically assumed it hadn't gone that well. Nothing could have been further from the truth but as so often with Anthony he felt no compulsion to speak of it, it was their little secret, their love, their life.

Anthony Johnson

And indeed there was love, they would sit or lie, caressing each other arousing each other, gentle intimacy would turn into passionate sex. It was on this basis that they loved, they both had a deep, respect for each other, they both loved to love. So it came out Anthony had been reluctant to broach the subject, but now he let little things go. How his relationship with Emily had died on its feet. How he had put so much of himself into it and then nothing: He had felt bitterly let down.

For her part Lucy explained how she had become a divorcee so very young. The man who she had loved and married had failed to make her a woman that very first night of her honeymoon. He had seen a doctor Lucy had felt all the while it must be something wrong with her. In the end he wasn't man enough to tell her himself but she found out from another source: he was gay. He had only married her at the insistence of his father who proposed to disinherit him unless he could show he was having a "normal" relationship. When she put this to him he had begged her not to allow anyone to know the truth, as she said, "he must have really needed that money." Hence she had grounds for divorce that they had not managed to consummate their marriage. All in all it had made her very low, so she had gone into nursing, and if he must know, that was how he had come to find her at the church.

Lucy having spoken with such candour Anthony couldn't help but do the same. There seemed so much to say; about his father who he held in high esteem; about his brother whom he hadn't really felt close to since he left home; about his mother who still seemed the powerhouse that she always was; about his school life and his lack of ambition. It was that, his lack of ambition that she pulled him up over, what did he really want to do? She felt with such a broad education he could almost pick and choose. On his part he didn't feel that he could face going back to college. "Perhaps," said Lucy. "It wouldn't be necessary or maybe just part-time. The important thing was to look at his pluses. It was then that he made a little revelation he had in fact been spending the odd evening drawing and had gone as far as to buy some paints and other materials. It was obvious from Lucy's face she did not know how to take this, was he serious? If he was this could be make or break. She would have loved to have quizzed him, was he painting abstracts or nudes or, but she knew from his face the subject was closed, unless he brought it up again himself.

Anthony's attitude to art was pragmatic, it was simple really if one wanted to be a painter then the first thing was then to paint. Secondary matters over the use of colour or the representation of form would only then follow. The most important thing appeared to be the application of paint, without that there was nothing. Anthony had originally taken it up as perhaps his mother would have knitted, as something to pass the evenings. That was until he found himself working past midnight.

Anthony had started, not unsurprisingly, working from a calendar of picturesque Irish landscape scenes. From the outset he had a good feeling about what he was doing. He would apply the first brush full of colour and it would leap off the canvas, more paint was added and by degrees slowly he would allow the whole to lie down. It was as much a mystery to Anthony as to anyone else the process that led blank canvas to completed landscape oil. No sooner, however, had he found a way of working than he felt again that burning ambition to start something fresh. So turning to a sketch pad he began outline the substance of a nude. Unable to help it, his mind immediately leapt back to Emily, and there he found the voluptuous curvaceous folds of flesh that would so delight his pencil.

One cannot imagine the excitement that Anthony found in his new interest and perhaps as one might expect his life again overflowed and he was in danger of losing his job. This time, however, he was prepared and handed in his notice in full knowledge that he had sufficient funds behind him to be able to manage for the time being. Seeing as everyone was either unemployed or being made redundant in the current climate, one more wouldn't really make any difference at all. O.K. Supplementary Benefit didn't exactly allow for those little excesses but with what he had put behind him Anthony felt he would probably be able to cope.

David, at first quick to point out that nothing had really changed at the factory, later felt honour bound to admit that in fact they had, and left six weeks after Anthony. David wanted more than anything to earn some money and although looking for work in the current climate would be difficult if not almost impossible. He had had enough of working at the packing factory and as he would say later but for Anthony and his passing interest in Angie there was very little there to interest him.

Lucy, the one remaining working party of the threesome, was careful not to rub it in particularly with Anthony. She encouraged him greatly. So much so that he decided to attend some courses. First things first he'd have to turn amateur part-time painter into full-time artist if he had any hope of succeeding. Fanatical as he was about figure drawing and painting he enrolled on an evening course, this wasn't university, but it was a step in the right direction. Just on a whim he also began a two day a week course in Furniture making, everything from settees to dining room furniture from cabinet making to fabric design. In all honesty Anthony felt Lucy's confidence in him as an artist was somewhat misguided, although he knew she would love to prove him wrong. Looking forward himself he felt perhaps cabinet making might lead to something.

The very idea of furniture restoration intrigued him; he was fascinated by the idea that every maker had his own recipe for French polish; it was the individuality that marked each persons work that made it so exciting. Anthony soon found that when he was in the workshop time would fly by and no sooner had he started than he was finished for the day. Perhaps, this over and above anything else signalled Anthony's interest and commitment in what he was doing. He could already see himself working in a small workshop, running his own business, doing some restorative work and some original.

However he was also making gains in Art and what had started as no more than a hobby now became hard work. He had originally joined the class somewhat speculatively but his tutor had not bullied him, or run him down, quite the contrary, he showed patience and genuine interest in what Anthony was doing. So it was that the end of term came and the students were going to put on a show. Anthony discussed with his tutor which of his many sketches and paintings he could perhaps offer to exhibit. Imagine Anthony's joy when a member of the public offered to take one of his reclining nudes off his hands and this would be for a fee. Perhaps he had been wrong and Lucy had seen a hidden talent he didn't know he had. This was encouragement indeed.

A year or more had passed and Lucy and Anthony's relationship seemed as steady as ever; they both maintained flats of their own, they both enjoyed their independence. It seemed that all the encouragement Lucy had given Anthony was now beginning to pay off, and although she would not admit it she couldn't help but have an air of "I told you so". Also aware that this could be the tell tale signs of something more serious she had also managed to make Anthony at least moderate his drinking. To say that Anthony's and Lucy's relationship was based on a clear understanding of each others needs and feelings is almost to denigrate the wealth of experience that each one gained from the other. Strangely, perhaps, Anthony still held out against starting a full time university course, even though he had probably completed a sufficient body of work for entry into a college or university, his mother would have called him lazy, but in a funny sort of way Lucy somehow understood.

Meanwhile David whose gains and losses seemed some how caught up with Anthony, had started a job at the municipal library and whilst they no longer worked together this brought them closer than ever. David would tell Anthony all the gruesome details of his fling with Angie and didn't seem to notice that Anthony all but never spoke of Lucy and himself. It was with this back drop that something untoward occurred.

In fact it concerned David and Lucy rather than Anthony. Lucy picked up the phone - she hadn't been expecting a call and so it caught her a little off guard. It wouldn't have been Anthony because he was at his evening class. It was David. He wanted to know whether he could come over. Lucy didn't think any more of it after all they were all good friends even if David hadn't called round on his own before.

The first she knew of anything wrong was when she answered the door. Almost before she could open it, he pushed past her clearly he was very nervous about something.

"I've brought you some chocolates."
"Thank you." Lucy stood in front of David looking at her feet.
"You've got to understand" Began David again. "I can't live with myself its eating me up. I want you... and I have to know do you feel the same."
"I'll do my soul searching later but I am quite sure that I have never at any time given you the slightest reason to think that there could ever be any more between us. What I tell Anthony about this evening you will doubtless hear at some point. But for now I would thank you to leave."

David suddenly looked very sheepish and padded out of the flat as quietly as he should have arrived. For her part Lucy wanted to slam the door. After he had gone all her assertiveness and confidence waned and she found herself almost in tears. Damn men, damn David, damn Anthony damn them all. What had she done to deserve this? Better still what could she tell Anthony, that his friend and confidant was a liar and a cheat? On the other hand if she didn't mention it would that act as some sort of signal to David. What would she say? She couldn't imagine the words would ever come to her. Your best friend tried it on with me. And all that time David and Anthony had been friends how long had David thought of betraying their trust? Surely she could speak to Anthony but even then she wouldn't know what to say. It was times like these she felt the need for a silent confidant someone she could phone and just pour it all out.

Two or three days went by and for one reason or another Anthony and Lucy didn't get together, she almost expected David to put his oar in, but when she spoke to Anthony she soon realised he knew nothing of the events that had previously taken place. She had been over it in her mind a thousand times or more, but when she saw him she put her arms around him and felt like she could melt. She said nothing. Whatever David may of felt she couldn't put Anthony through her agony and had David ever showed his colours again someone would act. And then no-one could say what would happen.

One may have felt that it was not impossible that Anthony would have resented David's education and status; he was able to charm the pants off most people. But perhaps surprisingly any animosity generally travelled in the opposite direction. If David couldn't have it then he wanted it the more so, if it was there on a plate for him he could not show less interest or more conceit. Even with all this in mind it is almost impossible to imagine how he could have concluded that Lucy would have wanted any more than friendship with him. As perhaps she saw it, wasn't Anthony surely David's best friend. Had he completely lost his marbles?

Anthony remained ignorant of what had happened but wasn't he an injured party too. It was not untypical of Lucy that she would keep a lid on something like this, she was not a spiteful girl, and it was more for Anthony's sake, rather than any liking or loathing for David, that she did so. Despite this blip their relationship continued pretty much as it had done. What was so appealing was the way she was able to indulge, in a manner quite unlike any one else, to allow Anthony to feel that there was some growth or that in some way there was a learning experience that was ongoing. It soon became obvious that Anthony would pass his course in cabinet making and furniture restoration with flying colours. That being the case he would have the option of starting with a firm or alternatively setting up a small business of his own, reluctant as he was to admit it, the second of these two options was in fact the more preferable. What he was going to need however was a loan or grant that was sufficient to start up a business and sufficient to see him through if times were difficult. In order to do this he would probably have to go through the bank. With that in mind he attended a group of six seminars designed specifically for people setting up in small business. The next stage would be to draw up his business plan. It was to his credit that he was able to make a very small amount of money go a very long way. Eventually after a little reshuffling of amounts and business details Anthony opened his own workshop specialising in cabinet making and furniture restoration both new and old. It was not unlike jumping off the top board of an Olympic swimming pool; one didn't know just when one was going to hit the water.

Initially he didn't really take any orders but busied himself either restoring something he had picked up cheaply at a sale or building something from scratch. It is true to say he didn't really notice the passing of time, but as he went over his books he found that if anything he was a little ahead of schedule. However it was then that it started. He didn't really think anything of it at first. It was probably just something that he had eaten. He found himself running to the loo where he had violent and serious diarrhoea. Of course when it didn't pass he found himself going to the doctor.

To say the doctor he saw was unsympathetic would have been an understatement he was completely uninterested. He took out his prescription pad and wrote Anthony up for something but frankly Anthony had as little faith in the man as he had in his prescription. And when after another week he found himself not only suffering from the diarrhoea but also vomiting he felt his lack of faith was not unfounded. He went back to the doctor but by now Lucy was concerned and rightly so. If you have ever spent time with someone that is both being sick and suffering the runs you would know that in no time at all they become very thin even emaciated. Again the doctor tried to pass the symptoms off as irritable bowel syndrome, he even felt the necessity to mention anorexia. Lucy was angry in a way that I don't think Anthony had ever seen before, and she swore if he didn't send Anthony to see a consultant she would have him struck off. Reluctantly the old bird made a call to the hospital and an appointment was made.

When Anthony saw the consultant, a Mr, Giles, he was of no doubt that Anthony was seriously unwell and decided to have him in there on the spot. Although there seemed little reason for him to eat, as he was almost immediately sick again, meal times did at least serve to make a break in the day. Meanwhile he was not quite sure what tests they were running. Lucy would poke her head around the corner at the end of a shift and both his mother and his brother visited. Curiously David did not visit but Anthony found out later that he had a terror of being anywhere near a hospital.

There was all sorts of form filling to do they wanted to know everything from ones place of employ to ones next of kin, from ones religious beliefs to ones favourite food. The doctor came round flanked of course by a sea of students, they pushed and poked, and explained things as if one was absent.

Eventually the nurse explained it to him she seemed more concerned that he shouldn't eat anything for the next twenty four hours; he was having an op. She then explained a bit about anaesthetics and what would happen after he came round.

Before he could go into the operating theatre he would have a pre med that would probably be the last thing he remembered. In theatre they removed part of his gut and a part of his stomach, when he came round the doctor explained what had been done and went further to say that he hoped that would be an end to it. When Anthony had been home a few days he wrote to the consultant Mr. Giles to thank him personally for all he had done. He also changed G.P. When he was discharged from hospital he weighed little more than nine stone but the sickness and diarrhoea had stopped.

It goes without saying that during the entire episode his family had been besides themselves with worry and had waited all night for the results of his operation. Only then were they able to rest, it had been enough to turn them to drink. Lucy perhaps more medically equipped than the immediate members of Anthony's family had had to be consoled by Mrs. Johnson. It was then, some ten days after Anthony had come home that the body blow came. It was a

Anthony Johnson

Thursday and in amongst Lucy's ordinary mail was a telegram. It didn't really give any details but the message was perfectly clear. Her father had been taken seriously ill in Singapore; she was to fly out immediately. How he imagined she could just up root just like that it did not convey, and somehow she knew that her stay in Singapore would be longer than this cursory note at first suggested. With tears in her eyes and tears in her heart she spoke to both Anthony and Mrs. Johnson over the phone. But it was clear to Anthony that she might well be away for a considerable length of time. With this in mind he made an unprecedented move and decided to return to his parent's home in order to convalesce. I can't say Mrs. Johnson was happy with this because I don't believe she was, but I think she appreciated the delicacy of the situation even if she had turned a blind eye towards Anthony's affection for Lucy. Anthony on his part envisaged no-more than a couple of weeks under his mother's roof even if she invited him for longer and this, more than anything suggests Anthony's resilience and ability to bounce back. He was the optimist always expecting good fortune to appear on the most barren of horizons. So it was that he was the most unlikely character to suffer any form of depression, but it was with no other than that that Mrs. Johnson asked her G.P. to call on him.

She had given the nuts and bolts of the situation to the doctor over the telephone; how he would not speak for long periods; that he spent long periods in bed but then seemingly without rest or relaxation; where he usually had a good appetite he had none; and how he generally seemed apathetic and lack lustre. She did not go into more personal issues suffice it to say he had recently had an operation and perhaps that may have had some bearing on the situation. Anthony himself felt as if his mind had frozen; he could not smile, he could not weep, there was just that empty void, a cavernous expanse of nothingness. He would spend hours lying on the bed in part given up to day dreaming and at meal times he would show none or very little interest in his food. His brother was worried on the effect it would have on their mother. David felt partly responsible although that couldn't have been further from the truth. It occurred to Dorothy that had she been able she probably would have contacted Lucy but in fact Lucy had left no forwarding address and as yet she had not written. Strange then how such devoted friends could part.

Towards the end of the month a letter did come through, but it was as notable for its absences as it was for its content. It made no mention of her and Anthony's relationship, it made no mention of Anthony's illness, it didn't even really say much about her father and it was conspicuous by its brevity. What it did say however was quite plain and that was that she was expecting to stay on in Singapore. As Anthony sat and read the letter Mrs. Johnson watched as the clouds of despondency crossed his face. It was the last straw and Anthony found himself going into hospital like it or not. He was said to be suffering from reactive depression in so much as it was in part as a result of cause and hence effect.

It was a miracle to see the effect on Anthony after just a few days it was almost as if the threat of going into hospital had been holding him back. But it was obvious that any further improvement would not be as easy. I do not want to go into Anthony's hospital experience suffice it to say he was discharged on the basis that he would take up some form of sheltered housing. I think possibly Anthony's life had changed for ever.

On leaving his mother's, having fixed the fuse, she stopped him at the door and said, "Remember me to David. You two are such good friends."
And with that Anthony kissed his mother goodnight and headed home.

The following day and after an arrangement that had been made before the weekend, David turned up promptly on Anthony's door step at half past seven. After exchanging pleasantries the two became embroiled in a conversation that in many ways one might have felt did a little more than border on the bizzare.

"I could kill him," said David, in a voice that gave away little of the anger that he felt and seemed to express some kind of cool resolve.

Anthony Johnson

"He's sat down there, a couple of blocks away, smoking heroin, stealing stuff fo feed his habit, living off the state. It would be a kindness."

"Hang on, let's get this right, you have met or know of a heroin addict and you want to kill him." Anthony was neither condoning or condemning David, instead what he said was carefully metered to perhaps appeal to the little boy in him. Quietly he may have thought David, was just being a bit silly, mouthing off as he was prone to sometimes.

But then David said, "I am going to kill him, and not you or anyone else is going to stop me."
"Well wait a minute," said Anthony. "Surely if he's a heroin addict he is going to die anyway. And how can you justify murder, all the more you, your father was a doctor, surely he spoke of the Hippocratic oath and the sanctity of human life. Anyway what's this junkie ever done to you?"

"You don't understand," replied David. "He lives in a squat, he's dirty he never washes, but of all the things I hate him for by far the worst is because he deals. You don't know him, he doesn't just sponge, he profits from other people's misery to feed his own habit."

"In that case, if you feel so strongly about it, why don't you go to the police?" Anthony was learning all too quickly that he was running out of ways out and this was only serving to strengthen David's resolve.

"Frankly I would go to the Police if I felt that would be any sort of solution, but you yourself know they'd be very little help. They'd catch him with very little on him he'd get probation and community service, that's no sort of an answer."

"But frankly that doesn't justify you taking his life."

"Well perhaps you're right," conceded David at last. But then, "but I'm still going to kill him."

"I can see I'm not making any impression on you. But have

you thought about what you are going to do. I mean someone will find the body and then the Police will be involved and if you are not very careful you may find yourself with a lot more undesirables banged up, in prison."

"Yes obviously I've thought about that, and whilst there is always that risk it is a risk that I can minimise. I plan to go around there late one evening perhaps on the pretext of wanting to buy something."

"Hold on. What makes you think he will let you in? What makes you sure that he'll be alone? Don't you think he'll put up some sort of a fight. I just can't believe you are even contemplating this."

"Well that, my main line of self defence, is that nobody is really very likely to think of me as a suspect. After all I'm not known to him or any of his cronies and with a little bit of luck there won't be anything linking me to the crime."

"Yes, I can understand that but then I presume I am the only one you've spoken to about this and you are relying on me keeping my mouth shut." Slowly the mechanical wheels of Anthony's mind were beginning to crank into action. Initially Anthony had taken David's proposition as purely speculative, but while they had been talking he had realised that David was far more earnest about what he was about to do than Anthony had ever imagined. He had a sinking feeling that he may be about to be asked if he would provide an alibi. With this in mind he made and unprecedented step and asked David if he could go along with him. With that in mind the conversation ended and they agreed to meet up in a weeks time to discuss things a bit further as Anthony was at pains to point out there was no need to rush things.

Ridiculous as it may seem and with the benefit of hindsight Anthony would have done better to have never to have become involved. Unlike his friend David he did not harbour the victim any particular grievance. Hence he had entered into it really with only one thing in mind and that was to prevent David doing something that both he and Anthony might later regret.

Anthony Johnson

I think that David for his part genuinely felt he was doing society a favour and had David ever had to come up in front of a psychiatrist he probably would have told us that David had a fixation with death and drew excitement from playing god. The irony of course was that in fact Anthony had been up in front of the psychiatrist not David.

The victim, one Thomas Mann, of course was the third part of the equation. He also had taken a step by step approach to arrive at where he was; a junkie. He had started smoking cigarettes at the age of nine, either pinching them off a family member or if need be from the shops. At a little after his thirteenth birthday he had smoked his first joint and as can be imagined it was only so long before he made the next step to heroin. He had lived in the squat where he was now, no longer than a few months and with what he made dealing and his other income pimping the girl who lived with him he was well able to afford his habit. In some ways he was not the victim of events but there purveyor. This however was about to change.

Anthony had agreed to meet with David at the end of the following week, so for a little over ten days he was able to mull over in his mind how what had previously been unthinkable could now be averted. He thought about the morality of taking a life and whilst for Anthony that would have been important enough in itself, from hearing the way David had spoken, he felt it would have little effect on him. He had thought about the consequences of the killing. It was almost impossible to commit the perfect crime and so of course there was that risk that someone might put the finger on him, or there may be unforeseen witnesses. But as he went over the possibilities in his mind he always seemed to leave himself out of the equation, it was as if he didn't really exist. And then he was there at the final moment grappling with David making sure everything was alright.

They met as had previously been arranged but Anthony couldn't make head nor tail of the conversation it all seemed to go over his head. He wondered if he was looking at another bout of depression or perhaps he was going down with a bug such was his head state. As he sat there David's mouth was moving but Anthony was unable to focus on what was being said. Did he hear David say he had already done the dirty deed? No, that was just wishful thinking that would have left him out of it. The nightmare would have been over but he had heard wrongly and now David was outlining how they could go about it.

Confused and bereft of all sense Anthony wished David goodnight, his first thought as he went back inside his house was that he hadn't taken anything in the whole evening. Whether David had noticed that was in some doubt as he had followed the conversation on autopilot even having made the odd remark, but without knowing consciously what he had said. Strange then, that as he lay in bed that night the conversation came back to him. His starting point was when he had falsely believed David had gone ahead without him, surely it was at this point that in fact David was outlining what they would do. Again "they" it still sounded so unlikely and yet as it stood it wooed Anthony into actions, the consequences of which at this point he couldn't even imagine.

David had been saying how he would come over in the evening he would leave his van outside and whilst leaving the lights on in the house they would leave by the back door at about eleven thirty. It was only a very short walk to the junkies house and they would be back well within the hour. He could remember David saying at this point you are with me, aren't you? He had said he was, whilst secretly thinking to himself at what point it would be best for him to intervene to stop the whole stupid plan. David had also said how they would best be off wearing bulky clothing and that he would bring Balaclava helmets for them both to wear. Again at this point Anthony had felt that sinking feeling swallow him up, there was no doubt about it David meant business. All of a sudden a huge package of David's conversation came to him and was gone in the same moment without him being able to retain it, he did not know whether he was asleep or not.

About half past one he woke his body sweating as if it was sweating blood: he was drenched. He had dreamt that someone was in his room systematically wrecking it, breaking everything, and then he had made as if to call out but he could not raise his voice and with that he woke. Anthony was not a regular dreamer nor did he have recurrent themes in his dreams, but for want of comfort, as he lay there he tried to conjure up Lucy, but as he did so he seemed to see Emily, which took him back to a time before David, and perhaps for the first time there was a tiny seed planted which suggested that David might not be the fantastic bosom friend he had always believed. But no sooner did he arrive at this doubt than he allayed his fears reminding himself of the many happy times that he and Lucy had spent together. What he didn't like of course was what was happening to him, he could almost feel senses, his soul, his life essence, setting like a homemade jelly in the fridge and he was frightened. He was frightened should the Law come down upon him, he was frightened should his depression return, he doubted somehow that his intentions and feelings were being respected and in truth he knew that they were not.

David on his part was more and more gied up, he revelled in his chance to play God. He was self righteous above abusive, convinced that his actions would demonstrate how one individual could change societies misconceptions over its ability to act. Best of all he could see himself playing the part and that perhaps above anything else strengthened his resolve.

An evening had been fixed when the two of them would meet and pay Thomas Mann a visit. Had it been possible David would have liked a dummy run, almost as one has for a marriage ceremony, but for reasons of security he had decided that this would not be for the best. The last thing he wanted was an unknown witness putting him at the house before the thing was even done. Unsure of what preparations to make, if anything he was over prepared, if that is possible. He had stood in his room brandishing the weapon he was to use, he had been to a number of charity shops picking up various articles, some for himself and some for Anthony, but also some spurious ones just in case anyone followed his scent. He didn't have any particular reason for buying these clothes but were he asked he was sure he'd be able to think of some reason. When he went to buy the two Balaclava helmets he was at first so concerned that he even thought to go out of town, but pinching himself he decided to at least to try to be rational and bought them locally. As time passed he became more and more entrenched in his own rationale that Thomas Mann should die, and that he should.

When David had first conceived of this plan, well before that, when he had thought about death and how one could play a part in that, when he had felt the need to kill, he had by no means intended to rope in Anthony. He had felt he had been talking to him just as one talks to someone in the pub, never in a million years had he expected Anthony to throw in the towel with him. It was not that David wanted to brag about what he wanted to do, although it did annoy him that no-one other than Anthony had taken him seriously, but with a little luck this could play into his hands. If no-one thought he was capable of such a thing perhaps this was for the best. At least if the law did come sniffing around he was sure of a good character reference.

Anthony, for his part, might be able to sight Peter Finchley as someone that could vouch for his good name. An ex-copper, he couldn't have been better placed and Anthony also wondered whether he would get the low down on any police investigation, strictly off the record of course. On the other hand though, if he didn't pull his finger out for Anthony then he imagined Mrs. Johnson would have something to say about it. And unlikely as it may seem Peter could find himself castigated.

Had Anthony known how unlikely that was, or even, how unlikely his mother was to doubt her sons innocence, in this matter, I think he would have wept, both with relief but also with shame, in the knowledge that he could not live up to their high moral values. And indeed it was thinking in this manner that was slowly changing the way that he was thinking about his role in this instance. Little by little he felt less able to challenge David about what they were doing. His cowardice was more and more allowing David to assert his prejudices, determine what would happen, and turn Anthony from innocent by-stander to somehow being more involved. And perhaps because of his silence over the matter he was not in the same position as David, people did not feel he was so unlikely to commit the crime, it was just possible that he may. This in itself was a gross travesty.

Thomas Mann knew nothing of this of course, his life carried on much as it had done for many months. He would go out and make a phone call, maybe ask for a couple of bags, the man would come round with what he wanted, he'd peddle what he could and of course feed his own habit. His saving grace was also a close relative, that being his mum. Who although she couldn't get him in for treatment, still visited him. Sometimes she was seen at the house pleading him to let her in, sometimes they would go off in her car and he would come back cleaned up, obviously having had a bath and a decent meal, he was still very thin. His father had completely given up on him, which as Thomas saw it, was about the story of his life. He had left a job at a small engineering works, having taken early retirement with very good redundancy terms and now worked in a Tobacco and paper shop. Need-less-to-say Mrs. Mann did not bring her son home when her husband was about. Thomas had put enough strain upon their relationship.

When Mr. Mann did speak of todays youth, which was not that often, he usually expressed the view that they should all be given corporal punishment. And how in his day they learned discipline in the Army, none of this poncing about on the dole, you had to get a job or you wouldn't have any money. Somehow it failed to reach Mr. Mann that the Army didn't want them and there were two million unemployed, a good half of which were desperate for a job. Mrs. Mann had long since given up trying to explain to her husband that these addictions were seen as some form of mental illness, that did little to help the situation and only served to make it even more exacerbated. But for all this if Mrs. Mann had anyone to rely on it was probably her husband. And although his ways were from a time past, these had also been her times past and she could not help herself but feel that they had lived through better times than these, not worse.

Martin Williams

Alice and Henry Mann had initially both attended a meeting with the Psychiatrist, having had to wait six weeks after approaching their G.P. they were glad of this interview. However Mr. Mann later dropped out, he didn't want to speak of it but the Psychiatrist had hit a nerve and he was forced to blow his nose to stifle his tears. As he said later the doctor had been more interested in whether there was alcoholism in the family than finding out if he could treat Thomas. The doctor, Dr. Gately, had had to explain that in cases of addiction there was very little he could do without the patient's compliance. Unlike with other forms of mental illness he had no powers of restraint, as he put it he could not section the client. If Thomas was to be treated in hospital he would have to go into hospital willingly. Further he suggested that Alice might be able to attend some sort of self help organisation and there was of course both Alcoholics and Narcotics Anonymous. Perhaps Mrs. Mann would feel happier if she knew there were other people in the same boat, so as to speak. Mrs. Mann said it wouldn't make her any happier at all, and Dr. Gately suddenly felt very small.

In sheer desperation Alice attended some meetings but they did little for her and whilst she wrestled with her understanding of what she had heard called confidently an illness, she felt if anything more alienated not less. Thomas himself had been invited to see the doctor and to Alice's sheer delight and surprise he did turn up. although he vowed he would never go again. Dr. Gately was adamant not all was lost and expressed a willingness to see Thomas as soon and as often as he liked. Although had the truth been known in fact Dr. Gately was not particularly interested in this sort of mental illness and perhaps rightly would have reserved judgement on his ability to do anything to help. In fact in all honesty he may have felt that one of the private clinics might have been more appropriate although working in the national health as he did, he couldn't point this out.

Alice Mann, as with any parent in the same circumstances wanted bitterly to appoint some form of blame and was only too ready to find wanting in herself. Her husband seeing this in her tried to console her but knew nothing short of a miracle cure would help. Typically as months had turned to years Alice's conviction in her son had never waned and whilst she could not feel his illness she did somehow sympathise. Even her husband, not usually the easiest recipient of love and affection, had benefitted enormously from her grace and magnanimity. She was the eternal mother and wife and hence held her family in the highest esteem. Suffice it to say that neither parent could recall any instance of alcoholism or drug addiction in the extended family.

Perhaps it was actually Thomas' fault he had become a drug addict, though that in itself seems a little unfair. He had after all been introduced to drugs at an age when it would have peer pressure and a need to impress that were the governing processes in his development. Certainly I am loathed to see his parents as playing the guilty parts in his growing up. Right from the word go they had squandered nothing, always wanting the best for their child, allowing that child to grow up in the warm and comfortable environment of a loving home. And yet as he entered his teens they were both only too aware that something had gone seriously astray. It was, if credit may be given for such a thing, curious just how long Thomas had managed to keep his difficulties from his parents. But in the reverse of Anthony's life, where he almost could not bare to lie to his seniors, Thomas was excited by the web of deceit he was able to weave around him. And in the same way he was able to hide his smoking from his parents he later hid just how involved in drugs he was. If then he could hide it from his parents hiding it from the authorities would be even easier. The next obvious step was to be in supply, and perhaps this then was the beginning of the brighter side to his problems; not only could he fuel his own habit but he would have money in his pocket.

He had a girl living with him, but he was under no allusions as to what she wanted, but she had helped him get started, she was a few years older than he. When they had first met she had been on the game in fact she still was, perhaps when she was younger she may have been attractive but anyone who saw her now would know immediately what she was. Thomas didn't know it but in fact she liked him above and beyond what he could do for her. He was never violent, and although he could get angry he would just shout, or if he was in a real strop kick the furniture, but in all the years he had known her he had never started on her. That was rare. But then it was true Thomas suffered from that bizarre affliction compassion. His girl he knew had gone too far, there was nothing left in there any longer. Yes the mind and body seemed to work on some sort of basic essential manner but it was almost as if the working had been torn out, you knew when you looked in her eyes she had long since departed for never never land. What David thought comprised a heroin addict was some how bound up in Thomas' girl, though Thomas himself had been more careful. He still had a sensation of euphoria as he made his first hit, he wanted quality stuff, he weighed out little packages which either he or one of the others would sell on. But sadly the thrills and spills of life were subjugated for the high of a hit.

In his own mind Anthony had convinced himself that David would not actually go through with it. He had decided that their conversations on the matter were largely bravado and that David had no more idea of completing the task than Anthony. He just couldn't see it. David came from a good family background, if nothing else surely his period at university must have taught him a degree of integrity. Anthony had wanted to phone David just to make sure, but as the week went on he had felt more and more apprehensive about doing so . What if David did want to go through with it, what would Anthony do then. In his confusion he became increasingly frustrated and this in turn damaged his confidence and ability to act.

In contrast David revelled in all of this. He felt like a champion, here he was, making his mark, striking out at the evil in society. I don't know how long David had harboured the thought that he could commit the act of murder, what I do know is that he was almost fanatical about its execution. It soon became apparent that in his mind he had been making plans for a very long time. When he made his move it would be premeditated murder, not manslaughter, not a crime of passion, his rationale would not be in doubt.

Anthony Johnson

Thomas Mann would be in his house (although you can hardly call it that, it was a squat) between the hours of eleven and midnight probably on his own, of course there was always the off chance that someone might just call round but in fact that was somewhat unlikely. It would be an ideal time to catch him off his guard. And if he didn't want to let them in, the door of the squat was sufficiently flimsy it could just be kicked in. His girl would probably be the first to discover the body returning after her night on the streets.

From then on one imagined the police would be involved. They would be doing their forensic tests and establishing what time the victim had died, because David didn't envisage getting rid of the body; that was all part of it, that the body should be found. All part of making his statement. He had no feelings for those Thomas would leave behind, their sense of loss or grief would be as nothing to him. He would be left feeling empowered.

On the Thursday as had been agreed, David met Anthony at his house. He had brought some clothes which they were both to wear, he would burn them later. That would at least make forensic's job no easier. As they were changing again Anthony would have loved to say something but the look on his friend's face was more determined than ever. Perhaps he would say something as they were walking over to the squat, that wouldn't be too late.

Anthony and David left the house by the back, leaving David's van in the front and the lights in the house still on. There was a little lane at the back and although David was anxious to press on eventually Anthony felt bound to speak.

"Tell me you won't do it. You won't actually kill him. We'll just put the frighteners on him, maybe push him about a bit, give him a beating. But you won't kill him."
"Oh, come on. We don't want to be out of the house any longer than we have to. You just leave it to me."
"That's just it. I couldn't let you kill him. You do that and there will be trouble."
"Don't worry I'll see to it."

David, all too conscious of the time elapsing, pushed on quickly, followed at his heels, more and more reluctantly by Anthony.

Eventually they reached the door of the squat and David banged on it loudly. Just as planned Thomas came to the door and with that David pushed him into the hallway. Before Anthony could do anything David produced a large adjustable spanner and brought it down upon Thomas' head. One blow would have been enough but as Thomas fell to his knees David hit him again. There he lay, a hole in the side of his head, shivering as the last vestiges of life left him. In almost clinical interest David bent down and felt for the pulse in the jugular, there was no doubt about it Thomas was dead.

Meanwhile Anthony had gone white as a sheet. He had wanted to call out but had been too frightened. Now he looked at David but not his face but his hands and clothes, he was covered in blood. Then he looked at himself he too had blood on him. Quietly, he mumbled, "What have you done?"
As he looked on David appeared to be saying something, he could see his mouth moving but he could not hear the words. Then he realised he was beckoning for Anthony and he to leave the scene of the crime, and return home. More than anything Anthony wanted to grab David by his lapels and scream at that face, but such were his feeling of anger and resentment he had gone past that stage. As he tried to make his way towards his house his legs felt heavier and heavier he was afraid he would have to stop. And all the while he could see Thomas' caved in head lying on the floor his blood and guts everywhere. He should have warned Thomas, he wasn't responsible, David had done this, was he an accessory, he surely hoped not.

When they arrived at Anthony's house, again David was immediately very practical, insisting they take off all their clothes just inside the doorway and bundling them all up and putting them, in a black plastic bag which he would take with him.

Anthony Johnson

Even though Anthony's horror at what David had done was only matched by his reluctance to being left alone, he still couldn't get rid of David quickly enough. The long and the short of it was that he was now frightened by him. His fear of him lay not in his ability to do this thing so much as the complete lack of emotion he showed having done it. Whilst Anthony was almost beside himself with regret, guilt and horror at what had happened, David in contrast seemed almost happy with what he had done. He bundled up the clothes that he wanted to take home with him, washed his hands and face in the kitchen sink and offered to fix Anthony a drink. For his part Anthony remained transfixed staring in disbelief at his hands. David's way made Anthony think of his spell in hospital, he was in some ways vaguely reminiscent of one of the charge nurses, going about in his usual manner regardless of the mayhem around him. And again Anthony experienced the chaos he had felt when he had been admitted for treatment in a psychiatric hospital.

"For Christ's sake," he muttered under his breath and with this Anthony took a large mouthful of scotch.

Over at the squat things hadn't really started yet. Thomas Mann deceased, lay on his own, his eyes staring endlessly up towards the ceiling a horrific picture but one that he knew nothing about. The blood was not now spilling from the wound in his head and some of it had begun to congeal on the carpet. It was not until nearly half past two that he was finally found.

Emma, Thomas' girl had tired of doing her round on the street earlier than usual that evening, it had been a quiet night and frankly it had turned cold. Despite her position on the social ladder she could still be head strong and that night she had got it into her head to go back and see Thomas, perhaps see if she couldn't get a little pick-me-up.

As soon as she arrived she knew something was wrong, the front door was half open and it being a cold night that seemed odd. She stepped in and had to put her hand to her mouth, she was going to be sick. She was still racing to the kitchen when she started to vomit, but not really having very much in her stomach she stood bent over retching. If there was one thing that she would never forget about Thomas Mann's body it was his eyes, they were the eyes that led you to his soul and said everything about the way he had died violence was inherent. In her panic she wanted to lay down beside him and snuggle up to him, offer him some consolation as if he was still alive. But the sight of him was abhorrent, ghastly, deathly, even in death he had not found peace.

She knew she should contact the police, but as thoughts raced through her mind, she wondered how she would explain his use of drugs and her little number on the game. Perhaps with the seriousness of what had happened they would overlook that.

Had Thomas forgotten to pay for something he had had, was this a gang land killing, had some other crazed addict caved his head in. The possibilities were endless. Would they come back for her. Suddenly she felt very afraid. Could she just pick up her things and leave, disappear into the night, but she could not leave him here like that. Should she contact a priest or ring an ambulance not that they could do anything for him now. She went upstairs, his room had not been disturbed, quickly she started searching, there might be some money or if not perhaps something she could take. Then she realised there was no time left she would have to act. As she passed the body it reminded her of how cold it was outside and she wrapped her overcoat around her as if she was shivering.

As was so often the case Alice Mann lay beside her husband in a light doze, half awake and half asleep. For his part Henry was snoring, not loudly, but rhythmically almost wooing his partner to do the same. Alice Mann sat up alert and awake she had realised the phone was ringing. She threw her dressing gown around her shoulders and casting a look across the room at the clock went down to answer, imagining as she did that it would not be an emergency she was prepared to fly into a rage. As she put down the phone the grief she felt at losing her son was immediate, all of a sudden she felt very alone, there was no quick fix she had all the time in the world, it was over. She did as she had promised and phoned the police - she could understand why this was difficult for Emma but had asked her to stay with her son, at least until she was able to get there herself. Half an hour later she was still sat in the kitchen in her dressing gown sipping a hot cup of tea. By God when she got her hands on the people responsible for this she would make them suffer. Truth be told she was almost reluctant to wake her husband, she had had all the dealings with their son, yet she knew that it possibly would hit him the hardest, unlike her he was not prepared, Alice had secretly always feared the worse.

Within the hour Alice and Henry Mann found themselves outside the squat where their son had lived. The police had sealed off the crime scene and the body was on its way to the morgue or at least that was the way the police officer had put it. Emma had been taken to the station although again the officer was at pains to point out that she was unlikely to be charged, at least not with murder. It was late and they might as well go home they wouldn't begin questioning until the morning and then they would make a house to house, they knew where to find them if there was any developments. But they would be needed to identify the corpse, but again that would wait until the morning.

The following morning it was Alice Mann that went down to the morgue to identify the body. Strictly speaking it should have been Mr. Mann that should have gone as he was the next of kin, but Alice was all too readily aware of the effect Thomas' death had had on him. So she went herself.

She was accompanied by a police officer and although she thought she had prepared herself for the worst, when she saw her son laid out on a morgue trolley nothing could have prepared her at all. As she saw his face she let out a silent scream and burst into tears, as she turned away from the body she lent heavily on the officer's arm and wept into her hanky.

"You will get the people responsible for this?" She half

asked, half demanded.
"You can rest assured, everything that can be done will be done." Replied the officer. She repeated herself.
"You will get the people who have done this to my son?"
"We have started questioning people and our investigation is underway. You can rest assured we will find out who did this to your son."

Now that the body has been identified, the next step was to mount a house to house. Officers would knock on doors, perhaps someone would have seen something from behind a curtain, perhaps someone would have noticed something unusual in the street that night. However as they started their investigation they quickly realised that for the most part the surrounding community would be of very little help. Even if people in that street knew anything of that night's events they were very unlikely to say so. To say that Thomas Mann and his moll were unliked would be to speak of a travesty of such magnitude it was almost unthinkable. Whatever else people felt they were glad to be rid of him, perhaps now the council would do something about that squat. What they of course did not know was that the council's hands were tied. They would have all to readily slapped a compulsory purchase notice on the property had it only been possible. As the police made their enquiries they found increasing animosity towards the victim and a stony silence about its perpetrator. Frankly the police felt that even had anyone known anything about the incident they were very unlikely to say so. That was until they knocked on the door of an old man who lived half a block down from Anthony, a Mr. Petrelli. Of course Mr. Petrelli did not know who was behind the murder, but he was one of the first to speak openly about Thomas Mann's death.

"Yes, Thomas Mann, he lived in the squat a couple of blocks away. He wasn't a very good person, but I didn't dislike him. Sometimes as I worked in my garden he would walk by, he would say hello."

"I didn't want to get up on the wrong side of him," Mr. Petrelli continued.
"I think he was in some kind of trouble." And with this Mr.

Petrelli touched the side of his nose as if to indicate it was a some private business. "I don't know but I hear that there is something that is with drugs. Then I don't really want to know."
"You do know Thomas Mann is dead," said the officer in uniform.
"Dead, you say. Tom is dead. Oh that is not very good. Especially for him."
"Yes we are making inquiries, we believe his death may have been unlawful."
"It wasn't by his own hand then."
"Suffice it to say we think another party may have been involved. If you know anything that would be of help concerning his death or if you hear anything, you would let us know."
"Why yes. Of course officer. There is perhaps something. Him down at number Thirty Two he may know something. Not that he has anything to do with drugs but he may know something all the same."

The officer called at two more addresses with no avail, they had already gone to work. But when he got down to number Thirty Two he noticed the curtains were still drawn, so it was that he didn't really expect a reply, thinkng the occupant was probably away. To his surprise Anthony Johnson answered the door. Anthony looked ghastly, something that the officer noticed immediately. Anthony had spent the rest of the night after the murder drinking. He had drunk and then remembering what had happened he had been sick, retching over the toilet seat aware that there was no more to come but still retching.

"Good morning, Sir," said the officer. "I'm making house to house enquiries about the death of one Thomas Mann."
As the officer said this Anthony could feel him look deep into his soul, he would lie he'd had to lie and if he could lie convincingly that would probably be the end of the matter, at least for now.
"I'm sorry officer as you can probably see I'm a little under the weather. What was the name again?"
"Thomas Mann."
"Is there any reason why I should know that name?"

"Well not necessarily, but as you can imagine we are making routine enquiries in the area."
"He was a local man then was he? I'm sorry it doesn't ring any bells."
At this point the young P.C. would have loved to have quoted Mr. Petrelli but instead he bit his lip. Mr. Petrelli had been sure Anthony down at number Thirty Two would have known something and yet here he was denying all knowledge of the man and looking like death warmed up. Who said house to house and community policing was a waste of time. And with that the officer wished him adieu.

It did not occur to the officer who had made the house to house inquiry to go straight to the detective in charge of the case with the incongruity that he had found in the stories of Mr. Petrelli and Anthony Johnson. Suffice it to say he made out his report and filed it. If Detective Inspector Harper, who was leading the investigation, or anyone else for that matter, wanted to read the report well then all he had to do was look up the correct file. This did not amount to insubordination but the contempt with which the uniformed officer held the Detective Inspector was all too apparent. D.I. Harper did not really have his heart in the matter himself, he had countless murders, robberies, thefts and muggings under his belt, and the death of a heroin addict did not figure enormously in his general work load. Heroin addicts did die, they overdosed, their lungs filled up with fluid and they drowned. It didn't matter to D.I. Harper that this one had his head caved in and that they were looking at premeditated murder. He'd look over the forensic report, run a brief check to see whether this crime matched any others in the area and by then it would be almost lunch time and he could go down to the canteen and fill his belly.

For her part Mrs. Mann could almost smell the air of contempt and disinterest when she visited that station later that afternoon. Emma was still being held at the station, apart from being a whore and a heroin addict herself, she was also a key witness. Mrs. Mann could sense, if nothing else, how the officers felt that she could have done better. Emma for her part was coming down, and quickly, and it didn't seem to matter how much she craved they wouldn't do anything for her. She would tell them anything for a fix and it was obvious that whilst they could prosecute her, there was little likelihood of her being any use as a witness.

For her part, Alice agreed to answer some questions that wouldn't be put to her by D.I. Harper. But being forced to answer questions that she had no idea about made her feel like she was more of a culprit than the killer. They wanted to know where Thomas had bought the heroin he had been peddling. Did she know Emma was on the game? And a thousand other questions that she could no more answer then these. At one point she had turned to them and said, "Do you consider my actions criminal, because that's what you are making me feel? As if I had done something wrong and now I am responsible for my son's death. I can't answer you're questions, I don't know the answers." And again she was very close to tears. The interviewing officer replied coldly, "I am just trying to establish the facts."
"I loved my son, officer, and even though he broke the law I couldn't see him go to prison, even now I wouldn't have wanted that."

She didn't know it but in fact she was an accessory to the fact, in so much that she had allowed Thomas to trade in a class A substance. However it was unlikely that she would be charged, the police showing the better part of discretion. When she arrived home that evening she was exhausted past the point of tiredness and whilst she would have loved to have just got into bed she fixed herself a drink and prepared to face husband.

At Anthony's it was Thursday again, a week after the murder, and the phone was ringing. He knew who it was, it was his mother that was calling as she had done on the previous day and the day before that. Reluctantly he picked up the phone.
"Anthony, is that you? I've been trying to call you for a couple of days now and couldn't get you. Are you all right?"
He wanted to say he was fine and there was nothing to worry about, however.
"I'm sorry," he said. "I've been a bit under the weather. I think it may be my old problem again."

"Have you been drinking?" She asked.
"Yes, I think I've got my trouble back."
"Do you need to see a doctor?"
"Well maybe."
She wanted to come over to his house to see for herself, but he wouldn't let her do that, so he agreed that he would come to her. His house was a complete tip, there was dirty dishes in the sink and the general grime that accumulates when someone really doesn't look after themselves. He had not washed in days and the smell of sweat on his body was only superseded by the stench of spilt booze. He had spent most of the previous day and the day before that sat in an armchair drinking heavily. All around him was the litter of his excesses. He had not changed and his hair was thickly matted, where he had not washed it. Yet almost immediately he felt better for taking his mother's call. He still didn't see to himself however and left his house as he was, his mother would know what to do.

As he rang his mother's doorbell he almost immediately felt a sharp twang of regret. Why hadn't he tidied himself up? Surely she deserved better than that. Oh yes he remembered he had wanted her to know he was unwell, well that wasn't unforgivable. The door opened and he stepped right in.
"Oh, look at you," said his mother. "Whatever's the matter?"
"I'm sorry I've been unwell."
"You can say that again."

Mrs. Johnson who had never lost her nursing sense put the kettle on and made certain that he had clean clothes and took a bath, only then would she talk with him.

The first time Anthony had been taken ill with this degree of depression Mrs. Johnson had known immediately what was wrong with him. For although she had always nursed in general medicine she was none the less aware of fellow nurses that had gone into psychiatry. Never the less she was still very surprised and shocked to find her own son suffering from this form of mental illness or for that matter any form of mental illness. Whatever else she thought about her son he had always seemed a confident, well liked lad, who if he applied himself could have been successful in any number of well paid employs. The fact that he had not really applied himself she now saw in part as forgivable, as any parent may, she wondered at what point his current crisis had become unavoidable. Perhaps in psychiatry the chain of events that link cause with effect are more complicated than one can imagine and hence nearest and dearest can end up blaming themselves.

Once again she knew her son was unwell, her natural maternal feelings plus her determination to nurse her son meant that she had a set of clean clothes for him, she had taken away his others when she had managed to convince him to take a bath. She also prepared a more than ample meal, which they both sat down to eat and she had invited him to stay the night, something which he declined. Despite Anthony's reluctance to talk she kept a veritable barrage of conversation going none of which was particularly important, none of which he would ever be likely to remember.

As he was going back to his own house for the night he could choose either to take the late bus or to brave it and walk. Although it was a good couple of miles or more Anthony was certainly capable of walking it and in his current state of mind quite able. However, and largely at the bequest of his mother, he left early enough to take the bus. It wasn't until he was getting off the bus that he had realised just how much the effect of his mother upon him had done to allay his fears. He was living a nightmare but he may have felt a little of the burden had been shared.

As Anthony came round the corner into view of his own place he noticed a small group of young men standing by the side of a lamp post. They had their backs to him and whilst paranoia was not a word unknown to him Anthony did his best to ignore them. But as he approached one of the group turned round as if to speak with him. All of a sudden he found himself on the floor. He had been punched in the stomach which had made him double up, a knee had been brought up and smashed into his face. He lay bleeding on the ground. All of the men were involved now, kicking him again and again. Desperately he tried to conceal his face and front by curling up into a ball, by now he knew these were friends of Thomas'.

One of the gang bought a heavy hobnail boot down on his leg as he lay there. His leg broke. Then two of them lifted him up by his arms and beat him again and again around the face. Whether they intended to leave him for dead is not clear, but a light came on in a bedroom window and the youths made off obviously not wanting to be recognised. As Anthony lay there an elderly man came out onto the pavement whilst his wife stood in the doorway.
"Call an ambulance," he shouted to her and then proceeded to do nothing except stand there and look at the mess that was Anthony. The ambulance didn't take long to come and because it had been reported as an assault a squad car also appeared and although they couldn't arrest anyone, for the second time within a fortnight they would be asking questions and taking statements.

When Anthony arrived at hospital his condition was described as serious but not critical, even so he found himself on an acute ward. Mrs. Johnson would have to be contacted as she was the next of kin, and through her David would also hear the news. Again David's dislike of hospitals meant he would not visit and he was also keen to take his absence, fearing for the worst that something similar might happen to him. Mrs. Johnson arrived at the hospital a little after one o' clock in the morning. Immediately she felt a strong impulse to take over her son's care, instead she had to bite her lip and put her faith in the nurses and doctors, as so many had done in her day. As time went on she became increasingly worried but eventually the doctor appeared to speak with her.
"What can I say?" Said the doctor. "He has multiple fractures in both his legs and his ribs, he has a broken nose and a broken jaw and his eyes are so bruised it is impossible to say at the moment whether he still has his eye sight."
Mrs. Johnson put her hand to her mouth as if she was going to be sick.
"My God!" She said.
"Despite that he is awake and his condition may be described as serious rather than critical. If you want to go in

to see him, you may."
"Why yes. But do we know what happened, or who has done this?"
"I'm afraid that is not my concern, and to find out more you will probably have to contact the police. If you will excuse me." And with that the doctor made off.

When Mrs. Johnson went in to see her son she had been prepared for the worst, but peculiarly, despite the pain he was in, he was in a better state than possibly she could have hoped for.
"Is that you mother?" He asked as she spoke to him. It was his habit to use the word mother rather than Mum whenever he was in trouble. She didn't know what to say to him, when in fact anything would have done. She held his hand.
"It's alright darling," she tried to comfort him. Her sense of maternal instinct was greater than ever.

The police car had followed the ambulance to the hospital, it was strange that this area of town was suddenly in the limelight, they would go months without any serious crime and now within the space of a couple of weeks there had been a murder and now this. Even the densest police officer was bound to ask if they were related. They were hoping to get a statement from Anthony but as it was the doctor managed to get three days before Anthony would make any comment about what had happened.

When he did so he was again compelled to lie and led the police to believe that it was probably a racially motivated attack, he had not known any of his attackers, that much was true. By now Detective Inspector Harper was aware of the house to house report that had been filed and whilst he had been furious that it had not been brought to his attention earlier, there was nothing he could do about that now. Did he have a suspect, albeit a suspect beaten to a frazzle, but never-the-less a suspect? He would have to go back and reinterview Mr. Petrelli perhaps this would add weight to his investigation.

As it turned out Mr. Petrelli did not really have anything to add, what is more, rightly or not, he was frightened. When another officer called upon him, he did not invite him in and furthermore said that he had had no real reason for thinking that Anthony would have been involved other than that he tended to be up on most of the gossip. Whilst being incapable of doing anything about it, the officer sensed he wasn't telling him the whole truth. But with little concrete evidence to go on there was little they could do.

About this time they also interviewed Mrs. Johnson about her son. She had initially expected the interview to be concerning his beating and at the outset they did nothing to make her doubt that. But as the interview progressed she realised that there was more to this than she had previously expected. They were probing her concerning Anthony's depression and she said that it was almost as if they saw him as a being at fault. It was then that the police dropped their bombshell.

It was obvious to D.I. Harper that if Anthony was to be considered as a suspect and then the only suspect, should his mental health be called into question, he would be unlikely to stand trial for murder. He was more likely to find himself guilty of manslaughter with grounds for diminished responsibility. That being the case he would find himself not in a prison but in a secure hospital, or on a ward within a mental hospital that was secure. Although that would rap things up it was not quite the same feather in D.I. Harper's cap. If possible he would really have liked to have gone for premeditated murder.

Three days had gone by and Anthony's eyes were now less swollen, thankfully he had retained his eyesight and his injuries had not left him blind. Never-the-less he had a leg in a cast, his rib cage had been bandaged and his jaw wired. Even in this condition the police were adamant they wanted to interview him and largely at the objection of the doctor's they were allowed to speak to only him briefly.

D.I. Harper would have loved to have thought that he had his suspect already to charge, however another problem had arisen. Speaking with the forensic pathologist it had become clear that it was unlikely to have been Anthony who had delivered the fatal blow, because the angle and height from which the blow had been delivered did not correspond with Anthony's general height and weight. A bigger man seemed to have been implicated. Putting this to one side, D.I. Harper still felt he was justified in pursuing Anthony as the culprit, in his view forensic evidence could be useful where it helped to convict the criminal it was less useful where it did not.

By now Mrs. Johnson had the information she needed about the police investigation. Peter Finchley, her friend who had relatively recently retired from the Force, had pulled a few strings, and was consequently fully aware of D.I. Harper's interest in the matter. Unlike D.I. Harper he felt that there was a good case that Anthony was no more than an outsider and was not that involved. And from the back seat of a bar near the police station he shadowed D.I. Harper's investigation.

Mrs. Johnson, as all mothers do, when faced with a situation that undermines their ability to protect their young, blamed herself for the attack on Anthony. Although there had been nothing she could have done to prevent it and whilst she knew it was irrational, she still felt herself to have been wanting. As to the suggestion that Anthony could have in anyway been involved in a murder, she thought that was plainly ridiculous. Even Peter Finchley with all his years on the force felt it to have been unlikely. At this point he required Mrs. Johnson to do two things, the first was to seek out adequate legal advice, the second was to ask the advice of his consultant psychiatrist. As it happened both would later be required in a set of circumstances that at this moment seemed almost impossible.

Meanwhile a search warrant was issued and Mrs. Johnson had the dubious task of taking the police over his property. She had known from the outset that they would probably want to do this and had consequently given up a day to clean the house from top to bottom. She didn't hesitate to tell the police that he kept it up fairly well together on the whole, even though, as she had first seen it, it had been a tip. Something which she would later admonish him over, for her part she could not imagine how anyone could live like that, certainly not her son.

Meanwhile Thomas Mann had been laid to rest, put in the ground, that is to say he had been cremated. Alice had not wanted a big ordeal, just a few good friends and the very closest of relatives. She didn't even want Emma there and conceded to allow her to attend only at the last instance and that because of something her husband had said to her. So it was a very empty chapel that said goodbye to Thomas Mann, only at Mrs. Mann's insistence were prayers said and a hymn sang. Whatever Alice felt about the life Thomas had lived, for her, all this could be rectified with the power of prayer, her husband was more sceptical. It was uncanny really how Thomas' death had affected Henry Mann because it sort of crept up and hit him on the back of the head, it had been a happy release, though woe betide anyone who said so. Further, the look on D.I. Harper's face sort of beamed an expression that said why the hell didn't you report it all to the law, perhaps then your son would still be alive today. This Mrs. Mann did not want to hear.

Over in the other camp Mrs. Johnson kept a regular program of visits to her son, quite often Mr. Finchley would visit with her. She had contacted the consultant psychiatrist that Anthony had been under and expressed a need for them to meet, and she had also been in touch with a solicitor.

The doctor was quite candid with her and announced that he had been asked for an opinion from the police. In all probability it would come out in court there were signs that led the doctor to believe that Anthony could be a danger to either or both himself and others. Mrs. Johnson was astonished, how could that be she had felt that the doctor like so many others would find her son a likeable lad. He had to be quite blunt it wasn't over whether her son was liked, of that he was fairly sure, it was whether her son posed a risk either to himself or others. Mrs. Johnson undoubtedly felt very very angry at the doctor's findings but as she left the doctors rooms she felt exhausted more than angry. Did no one other than her know her son? He was innocent she knew he was.

Anthony Johnson

The interview with the solicitor had proved similarly useless. Mrs. Johnson, although she had money, she still felt that to spend say three thousand pounds on a legal matter would indeed be to spend a very great deal. Even Peter Finchley, afraid of embarrassing her, dared not broach the subject. Suffice it to say there was very little the solicitor could offer to do for her; for the comparatively measly sum she was offering him for his services. Again she found herself all tied up in knots. She was glad at least that Peter Finchley had stood by her side, whatever else happened there was a rock she could fall back upon, and her gratitude belied the affection that she felt for him.

During their investigation the police interviewed the remainder of Anthony's family, in this group we may include Peter Finchley and the powers that be in his life, such as his G.P. psychiatrist and other professionals. They also interviewed David.

David could not have known whether Anthony had used his presence at his house the night of the murder as an alibi or not. He decided to hedge his bets that he hadn't and then later if he couldn't remember which night he had spent where it would not matter. True to form as the officer continued interviewing him it became apparent that there was not even a whiff of suspicion. That being the case he felt he should back Anthony to the hilt. In fact David was the sort of person that in later years we have come to regard as a pathological liar, he didn't only lie, he actually believed those lies to be the truth. So confident was he at pulling the wool over peoples eyes that even a trained officer of the law would not immediately see through him and so after a little over forty minutes the interview ended and David was left in the clear.

It was quite clear to D.I. Harper that before anything else was going to happen he would have to wait for Anthony to be released from hospital. Even then prosecuting for a case of premeditated murder was becoming more and more unlikely and if there was an acquittal then he really would be up the khyber. Given the circumstances even if he had a signed admission of guilt there could still be problems he was tempted for the good of everyone to cut a deal with Anthony's psychiatrist. If he did that the case was unlikely to come to court or if it did, no further than magistrates court, so that he could be held in custody. It would be less embarrassing for the doctor who would be able to refer him to a secure hospital and D.I. Harper could wash his hands of the whole matter.

That evening Peter was sat in his usual seat in the back of the Dog and Duck when one of the officers he had known in the Force came in. The news that Anthony was unlikely to be tried, he was more likely to be held indefinitely under a section in accordance with the powers of the home secretary regarding the seriously mentally ill, shocked him to the core. How the hell was he going to be able to break that to Dorothy. He wondered if D.I. Harper had ever had anything concrete on Anthony, or was he just doing his usual trick of passing the buck without ever really seeing the thing through. He thought to himself how surprised he was that nothing had changed and how obviously hit and miss the service provided by the police was. Thank God he was out of it now.

However brief, I do not think Anthony's arrest and detention should detain us for very long. There were perhaps some details of his appearance in the Magistrates court that may be of interest.

Anthony was brought to the dock handcuffed to an officer, having spent a couple of days in the cells. His appearance was not to be admired, despite his mother managing to get a suit to him, and one of the officers availing him of a razor. He found himself able to look completely unkempt and with his sunken eyes and thick furrowed brow, he looked every bit the part of a mentally unstable murderer.

As the magistrate entered court, the entire court stood, as they were asked to do so, that is excepting Anthony, who sat riveted to his seat. So phased was he by the whole experience that he could not move. Two court attendants made a move towards him but as the magistrate was almost seated himself he waved his hand and Anthony was not made to stand: at that point he did not really take part in the proceedings at all, it was only afterwards that he was able to remember some of what had transpired.

The charges were read out, manslaughter rather than murder, a reduced plea on account of the defendant's mental instability. Only one witness was called that being Anthony's psychiatrist, who after giving his name and qualifications, served only to tell the court that he wanted to detain Anthony on an acute ward of the local Mental Hospital, that being Hawthornes. The whole proceedings seemed to pass in an instant. Anthony was allowed to say goodbye to his mother on the steps of the court and was then whisked away in a police car, the whole unhappy matter had been resolved. All that remained was for D.I. Harper to inform the Mann's that their son had been murdered by a fruitcake. Although this in itself brought no joy to D.I. Harper he was only too pleased to close the case as he saw it justice had been done.

Although Anthony had been to Hawthornes before, the likelyhood of him finding his way onto the secure unit was as impossible then as it was now, and there were murmurings from the staff that they felt this was far from fair. As they knew Anthony he was always polite, he had never been violent, and in their hearts they felt some affection for him. He was, on a scale unprecedented previously in his life, completely broken hearted. Even his machinations over his relationship breakdown and subsequent unemployment following his affair with Lucy could not match how he felt now. The staffs kindness, though it wasn't meant to do so, broke his heart the further and he had to constantly check himself that he did not let the truth go. What ever else he did he would not squeal, and that David could rely on. Though whether David would have shown such resolve had he been in similar circumstances himself I somewhat doubt.

I would have liked to report that Anthony moved into the secure unit and found himself fairly settled; after all he knew some of the nurses from a previous stay that had not been on this unit. These nurses treated him well, although as I have said with a sense of disbelief. The nurses that regularly worked on this ward alone, were less compassionate. Anthony quickly isolated two of the inmates in particular that were going to give him trouble. Largely because of their size they were responsible for most of the bullying on the ward. If he tackled one of them then he would have much less trouble later.

Peculiarly the kicking Anthony had received made him more, rather than less, confident about doling it out, after all if any fight went as far as that had done then someone would be for the high jump. Officially there was not supposed to be any money on the ward, although small sums did sometimes change hands. The inmates were paid a subsistence but that was generally held by the nurses, they would then purchase items each client as required, this could be anything from toothpaste to tobacco, or even small items of clothing. Unlike a prison regime the inmates would generally wear their own clothes, although on this ward unlike any other, the staff wore uniform.

As I have said Anthony did not settle into ward life easily, not only was he suffering from one of his darkest depressions, he was very bitter about the outcome of his former friends endeavours. Further he felt powerless to effect any improvement in his present position and much as he would have liked to accept his situation stoically, this was completely impossible.

He found by freely agreeing to take his medication the staff soon became more relaxed about whether he had taken it or not. This played into his hands and he was soon able to make a little stock pile of medication, that with what he was able to purloin off other patients, would seemingly be enough. With suicide in mind, he swallowed as many as he could and went upstairs to lie on his bed. He did not hear voices but something in him told him he had done the wrong thing. As he might have described it a little voice said, "What will your mother think? She won't want to lose her son. what will your brother think? Will he assume you were guilty? They'll say you just can't hack it."
Then he would try and intercede from his own consciousness.

"You haven't got anything to live for anyway. You heard the judge you are to be held indefinitely."
So the two arguments carried on for over an hour and then reluctantly Anthony went downstairs to try and explain the situation to the nurse. He knew from previous experience just how embarrassing for the nursing staff this could be, it wasn't simply a matter of making him sick he would in all probability be taken to the Royal Infirmary.

When he had gone down to break the news to the nurses that he had taken an overdose, the first nurse he had encountered was a petite little nurse called Sam, who was younger than the average. She had promptly marched him off to see Staff Nurse Knightley, Elaine. You know how it is when you make a first impression of someone that then tends to stick. So it was with Elaine. One thought of a dour, austere strict nurse who had the unlikely attribute of a uniform that fitted. Where Sam was petite, Nurse Knightley was of a fuller figure, although she was not fat but shapely, I believe they would have said. Although she was clearly very angry about what had happened, Anthony had just the slightest feeling that in some respects she didn't blame him so much herself as the other nurses. After all had the outcome been different then there really would have been something to shout about, and in that respect she was almost thankful to Anthony. An Ambulance was called and for the twenty minutes before it came Sam and Elaine sat with Anthony and tried to placate him. Their kindness was such in regard of what he had tried to do, he was near to tears, he didn't know whether that was a good thing or not. Generally on the ward one tried to be as macho as possible, now he felt anything but.

He arrived at the Infirmary, a male nurse from another ward accompanied him, and he went straight through Casualty, for a moment he was worried that that was all there would be and that he would be rejoining his ward later that afternoon. What a joy it was then to hear the doctor explaining to the nurse that they would keep him in overnight, possibly even two nights, he was almost overcome with emotion, despite the nurse explaining that it was essential that he didn't abscond.

They pumped his stomach, an experience that was far less horrible than ever he would have imagined, and then put him on a drip. With the drip by his side he was wheeled over to the lift and then up to the third floor where he was to spend the night. Generally the average age of the men on the ward that he now found himself on was considerable, greater than his own, there was no smoking which came to Anthony as a relief, and he must have been the only patient that did not have his clothes in the box to his side. Although some of the other patients were watching television Anthony soon found that he was more tired than he had thought and slipped into a half sleep. Although he was hungry no attempt was made to bring him any food.

When the doctor appeared on the ward the following day, Anthony had had all he wanted of bed rest and almost wished he could return to Hawthornes. The doctor looked down at him and said,
"Well what have they been poisoning you with?"
To that there was no answer. Somewhat meekly Anthony replied,
"I've been taking antidepressants."

What Anthony had heard of the secure unit, whilst he spent a spell on Walker Ward, could in no way prepare him for the reality. Sure he had heard tales, of everything from anorexics being force fed to the staffs almost fanatical worry that anything sharp should get into the hands of the patients.

As may have been inferred Anthony was by nature someone that liked the outdoors. The secure unit allowed no more than an hour each day in the yard and while the yard did have grass it was no more than a small tennis court in size; and that surrounded by a high fence. It didn't take long for Anthony to become very claustrophobic. This was further augmented by the staff's almost religious concern with keys, to travel between two rooms one passed through at least two locked doors. In addition to this there were staff strategically positioned between the more major passages.

The staffs concern with sharp elements did not end with the

counting of cutlery that continued every evening and after each meal. There were constant room searches although these were not only conducted for the purpose of finding sharps. If ever a cup or plate became broken, by whatever means, the staff would come rushing in to rescue it before it was used to hurt anyone. One sometimes thinks they must have taken their life in their hands.

Tantrums were commonplace with some of the inmates. If things became violent then the staffs first concern was the threat to their own person, after this was their obligation to the patients. As much as he could Anthony would avoid coming into close combat, knowing only too well that they had the strength of a mad man. At the same time he did enough to make sure he was not bullied. Nigel Bradbury was not one of those who generally created a scene. He had been one of the first to welcome Anthony to the ward, but as he walked through the dining area having just spoken to the psychologist, responsible for turning round the minds of these psychopathic prisoners, something snapped.

Being accompanied only by a more junior member of staff, in part he was given the opportunity or at least that is how he would have seen it. Breaking away from her he let out a terrifying scream and picked up the object nearest to him, that being a table, and hurled it across the room. Letting out further screams and yells he pushed himself through the sea of tables and chairs, throwing each to his right or to his left. The nurse accompanying him paged the heavy boys on her bleeper and within no more than a minute or two, four of the largest men one could imagine, let themselves into the room through the locked doors. Satisfied that there was back up, if it was required, she signalled to these men to stand off for a moment or two. It was a courageous decision as the general rule was to wrestle the patient to the floor and then issue a heavy sedative that would all but knock a man out.

Sure enough Nigel had seen the heavies arrive out of the corner of his eye, and feeling that he had done enough to release his feelings and make his point, he stopped throwing the furniture around and stood for a second with his head bowed. Then his hand went up to his face and the nurse

could hear him sobbing, as she approached he said, "Why me? Why does she say such things? I haven't done anything to deserve it. Why pick on me? You're always picking on me."
At that point the nurse could not know whether this was a lull in his exertions or the end to them. As it turned out it was the end and although he still had to have his sedative in some respects the nurse couldn't help but think that perhaps a barrier had been crossed. Either way he would spend the next twenty four hours flat on his back. From the outset the psychologist, backed up by the nursing team were out to demonstrate to him that violence was not a means to an end, and although that may seem obvious enough to us, to Nigel, it was hoped that this might lead to the forming of a hitherto unknown rationale.

After an initial settling in period, Anthony just like everybody else, was put forward to receive Psychotherapy from the resident Psychologist. When he had been on the other ward, he had been almost informal and finding this process both painful and unhelpful he had ducked out. If anything previously the tablets had seemed the most useful of things.

The psychotherapist was a woman, and you know how it is when the very first time you go to see someone you don't take to them, so it was for Anthony. All Anthony could think about was that she was some kind of ex hippy who was probably vegetarian but ate fish and fowl. This could not have been further from the case, she was in fact a graduate of Oxford and was far too young to have been a hippy. Vicky, as she was called, could not really have been better placed to help Anthony, and although he didn't know it, she would be one of the first to question the wisdom of entertaining Anthony in a secure unit.

In the first few weeks of the sessions Anthony had with Vicky, she spent a lot of time talking about his family and ground with which he was fairly familiar. She found on mentioning his father, the first time, she cut him to the quick and generally when she reported back to the chief, she presented him as a sensitive young man. This she felt was important if they were not to break him, the consequences of so doing, she argued would be dire. Sometimes they would sit in silence, Vicky was perhaps waiting to establish where the session was going, Anthony for his part was composing himself. It was out of one of these moments of silence that Anthony began. "You know you said if I felt that I was finding it difficult to get on in these sessions, that I could if I wanted nominate someone else that perhaps would take up my counselling and therapy. Well I don't mean any slur on you but I wondered whether this would still apply?"

"Yes," mused Vicky slowly.

"The fact of the matter is that I get on very well with nurse Knightley, I feel there is some bond there. Not that I mean to demean the work that you've put in in any way, merely I wonder if I wouldn't find it easier to talk to her."

Vicky, Vicky Chandler was quite angry about this, but true to form she kept her calm, and reluctantly she agreed to look into it. At this stage neither he nor she could be sure nurse Knightley would even want to take it on. Even if she did want to take it on it would probably mean more work than less as she would have to have supervision, something that Vicky received automatically. At the end of the day she could not help but feel this was probably a mistake, but that was Anthony's perogative, and while she would voice her apprehension and dismay, that in itself would probably not be enough to prevent it from happening.

Frankly Elaine Knightley was chuffed that Anthony wanted her to take over his sessions. She had liked him from the beginning of his stay on the ward, furthermore she hadn't done this sort of work for quite a time. When her brother phoned from Australia, as he did at the end of every month, she was almost girl like with excitement; as both he and she knew only too well, she had a name for discipline, discipline and starched uniforms. For his part Anthony was pleased to be out of Vicky Chandler's hair and right from the very first session with Elaine he made it clear that he wanted to make a go of it. It was noted that he was becoming compliant. Even the consultant psychiatrist, a Dr. Alex Walker, but not the Walker that had given its name to the ward, was impressed to see how well things apparently seemed to be going, though he always held a little in reserve, for fate had instructed him to be cautious.

Elaine Knightley sat on a low easy chair, opposite Anthony, she had a bundle of files in her hands which meant that her eyes were diverted from his. He was adamant that he would not stare, or if he did he would not get caught doing so. He looked at her dark brown hair, that smelt of womanhood if one got close enough; he followed the flesh tones of her face and neck down towards her bosom, which was ample; he measured her waist as if with a tape measure. He looked up and met her eye, she had just that second stopped reading, he hadn't been caught.

As she began talking to him he just looked down, except he didn't just look down he looked at her feet. He did not cross his legs, but sat with his hands in his lap, like some Turkish wrestler sitting over his worry beads. He was listening intently to what she was saying, however whether any of it actually reached him, that I somewhat doubt. He felt again that strange sense of unreality, that events were taking place around him and somehow he had no part in it. Crucially it reminded him of the days and weeks shortly before the death of Thomas Mann.

Completely unaware of how long they had been sitting there talking, the session suddenly came to a close and it was only afterwards that Anthony was able to recall what had actually been said. Not to bore you with the details Elaine had covered much of the ground that her predecessor had, just confirming what she knew of Anthony's family background, his schooling and early life before he became involved with the psychiatric profession. Peculiarly he could not recall what he himself had said, although he was sure it was very profound, though probably not a great deal of help. Curious then that now Anthony would on the whole look forward to these weekly sessions, sometimes composing what he was going to say long before the session came round. And this more than anything marked a change in his thinking.

Anthony was becoming increasingly frustrated, why should he bare the lions share of all the guilt? Why should he be locked up in this God forsaken place? Why should David be at liberty to go as he pleased, when in fact it was him who had done this thing?

O.K. Anthony had been an accessory to the crime that he understood only too well, but what was that worth in terms of a jail sentence, perhaps four or five as a first offence, if he was willing to go along with the police and cooperate. Yet he was here and his term was indefinite, he could ring David's bloody neck. And this marked a change, he wasn't going to go telling tales, at least not yet, but his indifference towards David now bordered on antipathy. Still he bit his lip at the thought of a crown court judge sending him down for fifteen, twenty or more. In part these feelings were surfacing because of his better position on the ward, he now looked forward to his sessions with nurse Knightley and now sometimes he would dream, something he had not done for quite sometime.

The staff having noticed how he had begun to open up and maybe even trust them a little bit proposed that perhaps they could offer a carrot rather than the stick form of approach. So they left it to Nurse Knightley to establish how this could be operated. In one of their sessions following this consultation and as casually as she could she asked, "What do you miss most since you've been with us?" She half expected him to say sex or something like that. But he answered almost as if he had been ready for it.
"Sunday lunch. I really miss my Sunday lunch. Roast beef and Yorkshire pudding, Lamb and mint sauce, Roast Pork." For a moment Elaine didn't know whether someone had put him up to it, so she said, "seriously?"
"Yes, seriously. The food here, well it is edible, but the chef's hardly from the Ritz is he, now. Well there are other things as well of course, such as a half bottle of spirits, probably whisky or shaving unsupervised, but the one thing that really gets me is Sunday lunch."

When Elaine took this back to the other staff, she had already conceived of the possibility of taking Anthony over to the staff cantine. They did a Sunday roast and while it wasn't homemade it was a step up from the ward's. You can perhaps then imagine her anger when Dr. Walker completely slammed the idea as preposterous, she felt let down by the staff, she felt let down by Anthony and she felt she had let her self down. This however was not the end of the matter, peculiarly Vicky Chandler the Psychologist did not think this was such an outrageous proposal and said so. She could see how the relationship between Anthony and Elaine was developing and thought only good could come of it, she was not blinded by the acrimonious murder tag.

About this time Vicky took Elaine to one side, and spoke thus,
"It's not that Anthony is completely from the blame, there's no smoke without and all that, but I've been contacted by a Mr. Finchley, who is apparently a family friend and has known Anthony since he was a teenager. Mr. Finchley is also an ex-copper and so has contacts that perhaps any more usual member of the community would not, namely that he knows details beyond those that are usually released. He has told me that had the matter of Anthony's mental state not been in question, then the suspicion of murder would have been unlikely to fall at Anthony's feet. And the evidence, that the Police had, would have been unlikely to have been any more than circumstantial."

During the whole of this deliberation Elaine had sat quietly listening, only the slow look of horror as it came across her face, indicated this more sincerely.
"So what you are saying is that Anthony may actually be completely innocent of having committed any crime and only by the most dubious of circumstances finds himself here on the secure unit."
"That would appear to be so."
"Did this Finchley fellow give you any details?"
"Well yes he did, although at this point I am reluctant to go into them."

The conversation continued with Elaine saying how she had felt that there was something unusual about Anthony, something she had not been able to quite put her finger on. Vicky for her part was used to other members of staff feeding back their thoughts on any particular matter back to her. For both members of staff it was as if a great weight had been lifted from their shoulders and perhaps now for the first time they themselves wondered just what indefinitely would mean. After all if they were to make a good recommendation to the Board then perhaps Anthony would not be incarcerated any longer than was absolutely necessary, although they would probably have to convince several others of their feelings and that might not be so easy.

When Elaine and Vicky said their goodbyes there was a feeling in the breast of each that here lay a real opportunity to do some good, however difficult it appeared, to extricate Anthony from the system. It had also occurred to Anthony that perhaps this was the time to let a little go, he couldn't go on protecting David forever. David would have to make his move and get himself clear away from here, the responsibility for his safety could not be Anthony's. Hitherto Anthony had said nothing about what had happened the night they murdered Thomas Mann, not to Elaine and not to Vicky, he was not looking forward to discussing it.

Elaine, having cleared it with Vicky and a reluctant consultant, who felt it was all rather unlikely, agreed she would invite Anthony to join her at the canteen the following weekend.

Anthony knocked at the door of one of the offices they used for therapy and Elaine called for him to enter. He did so and sat down with his hands firmly rooted to his knees.
"I've been thinking," she said. "I was wondering about your request for a decent Sunday dinner." At this point she paused, and it was in the impetuous Anthony to turn round to her and say he had only been kidding, if he had had first choice of treats it would have more likely been a bottle or that more curious commodities sex. But he kept his peace.
"Well," she said. "I've cleared it with the powers that be and I can now cordially invite you to Sunday dinner with me over at the canteen.
"Alright I admit it's not the Ritz, as you have said, but I think you'll find it a bit better than the lunch on the ward."
"May I ask?" Said Anthony. "What is the prerequisite to being asked to lunch, because as far as I can see nobody else on the ward has ever been invited."

"You may," she said. "Although I'm loathed to tell you since we should have the whole ward over for lunch at the staff canteen." This she said so emphatically that Anthony could be in no doubt that the subject was closed. All that remained was to agree that they would meet after church and that Elaine herself would undertake to escort Anthony over to the canteen, obviously she felt confident that Anthony would not make any move against her, and her confidence was not betrayed.

Anthony had taken to going to church keenly and although he did not like the pastors constant badgering for those sinners to repent and seek the word of God, such faith as he had was well recompensed. In addition to his saying of prayers, in a hope that his guilt would be answered, he had also taking to bathing in very hot water, so hot that it scolded his whole body, but by this also he may have felt that he could expunge the devil. He was quite careful not to allow any of the staff to see his scolded body and although sometimes he would be in pain, he sat in his shirt and trousers, he never said anything. At times he would question the morality of taking up smoking, after all it was not only the other inmates that smoked, so did many of the staff; but usually it didn't take that long to convince him of the folly of this. Mid week he put aside a shirt that he could eat in that coming Sunday and hoped that the trousers he had would also not disgrace him. He would have done almost anything to get himself a tot or two of some strong spirit, but he was only too aware of the impossibility of this request.

As they entered the canteen Anthony was immediately struck by the sense of space and the light airy quality of the decor. Round tables stretched out over a wooden floor, all laid with knives and forks, side plates and dessert spoons. Due to the early hour in which they had arrived the place was relatively empty, they went along the food counter, with its assortment of cakes and sandwiches, and ordered a couple of cups of coffee. To Anthony this was simply heaven, fresh coffee, he had almost forgotten what real coffee tasted like. As they sat down it was Anthony that spoke first.
"So can you tell me, how did you end up with a name like

Nurse Knightley? Surely that can not have been by design, no-one working in your profession would have ever chosen it."

"Well no, you are right there. In fact my maiden name was Fairfax but I went on to marry a Mr. Knightley and just to put your mind at rest, there is no Mr. Knightley now. I have been a divorcee for quite some time now, although I still retain his name. It's a bit silly really, I could so easily revert back to my maiden name if I wanted to, but I don't want to."

Anthony may have felt this was a fairly brave statement coming as it did from a question that was designed to be flippant more than anything else.

"Your file indicates that you have been in hospital before, although I didn't know you then. The staff that did say you were in many ways quite different, true they remember you as polite, friendly and of a generous nature, and indeed they would have thought intelligent, although I don't know whether I should tell you that to your face."

Overlooking the fact that he was now described as being different from that he thanked her for the compliments.
"Well I did go through a period of fairly severe depression back in those days, when it first started I thought I was going to become suicidal, but thanks to the staff and everything."
"Yes," said Elaine. "The staff on that ward have said you responded very well to treatment, and that you were compliant, that being the medical term to say you co-operated."

"May I ask you," said Anthony. "What may I expect as a reasonable term in the hospital? I mean as far as I know I have been detained indefinitely, but that can't mean forever, can it?"

"No. I suppose in the case of someone like yourself, you might be thinking of perhaps fifteen years maximum, and maybe eight or nine as a minimum. Although after two years you will have the chance to put your case to the Home Office, who will in turn take their recommendations from ourselves."

"So you mean to tell me," continued Anthony. "That realistically I can expect to serve eight or nine years on the secure unit? That's impossible." Anthony paused. "And what happens if I die, not by my own hand, but if one of these morons takes it too far and kills me? What happens then? I suppose you will inform my mother and brother that I have suffered a tragic accident and that will be the end to it. No more Mr. Johnson."

"That is somewhat unlikely," it being Elaine's turn. "The staff keep a constant vigil of the going's on and the various interactions between both staff and patients. I think its safe to say you are in good hands. Though I appreciate your fears. After all if you hadn't been suffering from some form of mental illness you probably would have ended up in Prison, and that would not have been funny. And whilst I fully understand your anxiety over both the length of your stay and your circumstances during it, compared with prison I imagine this would have been a relatively soft option."

There was a carvery in the canteen and both Anthony and Elaine went for the beef.
"So you still haven't explained how all this fits in? Said Anthony, "I mean you asking me over to the canteen and everything. There's no doubt it will put my fellow inmates backs up for weeks, but that wasn't your motive I'm sure."
"Let us just say it concerned your assessment and leave it at that, shall we?"

"You know I didn't do it. Murder Thomas Mann, I mean." Then he mumbled under his breath, "I witnessed it though." It had been going round his head for weeks. "I murdered Thomas Mann," it said. Louder and louder, again and again, "You killed him." Talking to himself. "You were responsible, you didn't strike the blow but you were guilty by proxy. You murdered Thomas Mann. You are an accessory and you are guilty."

What about David then, "You've had your chance. You should have got away from here now. I can't explain it but I can't keep silent forever and once it is out it will be your head that's on the block. I hope you know that David." Again these thoughts went round and round his head like a whirlwind. He felt like a man who woke up every morning and spent eight or nine minutes banging his head against a wall, he thought about it so much it hurt.

Perhaps the thought of spending up to fifteen years on the ward would be the straw that would brake the proverbial camel's back. Or was it the increased feeling of loneliness and isolation, either way he felt he was going to have to tell someone what had truly happened, if he didn't he'd burst.

Elaine Knightley had turned up to meet Anthony in a navy blue trouser suit. As Anthony came out of church she was stood there waiting, she smiled broadly, and for an instance Anthony had felt like he was home from the Forces, as in one of those black and white War Movies about bomber command. He felt rather wooden and tried to force a smile that didn't really come off. If one had seen them walking down the path towards the canteen and had not known different one could have been mistaken for thinking they were brother and sister.

Likewise when they had left the canteen Nurse Knightley had suggested they take the long way round, a chance to take in some fresh air as she put it. Although Anthony was not tall she was smaller again, so that when one saw the two of them he in fact seemed taller than he was.

As they were walking along, she walked to his side, he could almost imagine her putting her arm through his, though of course she did not. Even though Anthony had made a personal note to take in what she was wearing, as soon as they parted it was all but forgotten. He now knew he had seven of eight years in this hospital minimum, he asked himself whether morally, he deserved that and curiously he was not at all sure he did not. Later that week Anthony was coming along a corridor where there was an office on the left, when who should appear than nurse Knightley, in her hand was a bundle of papers.

"Your mail," she said, pressing the bundle into Anthony's

hands.

"Oh, thank you," he said. "Here hang on its been opened."

"Yes, I'm sorry that's ward policy." And without another word she turned on her heels and marched off down the corridor. There must have been fifteen or twenty letters in the pile; if he thought about it long enough he could just about recall being told that he would forfeit his mail until such a time as his behaviour improved.

The wad of letters was not ordered in any particular way, so for the next few minutes he started shuffling them around, either in groups of letters that had all been written by a certain person or in some form of chronological order. Suddenly it became imperative to read as many of them as was possible in the shortest possible measure of time. This of course was not as easy as one was first lead to believe, the letters being largely hand written would take conceivably longer than was expected to complete.

I don't know why he ever would have doubted it, but immediately he was overwhelmed by the warmth of feeling contained in these letters, not a single one expressed anything other than his misfortune with the courts and their lack of belief in what had subsequently happened to him. Truly they all felt that had been a terrible miscarriage of justice.

Looking through the letters, at first glance, he thought to himself that those from his mother would probably prove the least interesting. However that was not the case and although he had to tease out the more meaningful parts from a mass of idle chat, even that was of interest, for example how his brother and various other members of the family were getting on. Centrefold was hers and everybody elses sheer sense of disbelief at what had happened and a general concern that they all felt, to continue professing his innocence. At the very heart of this his mother wrote that she had wanted to contact the Manns just to let them know that she in no way accepted the fate of her son and regrettable as it was that their son had died that hers was suffering unjustly. However on talking this through with Peter they had eventually both decided that this was probably to be less rather than more effective in securing Anthony's early release. All this was like a breath of fresh air to Anthony whose spirits rose within the space of an hour. If anything, it made him the more determined not to admit to his part in it or to implicate his good friend David, which had been in doubt over recent weeks.

The letters from Peter whilst obviously much more concise, dealt largely with what he saw as rough justice. As he saw it the police had done nothing more than to completely ignore the facts, in effect to achieve a quick resolution of what was much more of a serious problem than they had ever been prepared to admit. The evidence against Anthony amounted to no more than that was purely circumstantial, something most coppers would do best to make little judgement over. Because Anthony had a prescribable mental illness he was in short a soft target; the police wanted to deal with the whole matter as quickly as possible and then just forget about it. Rumour abounded that there had been some kind of deal and Anthony had been given the short straw.

Anthony wondered had the profusion of mail specifying Anthony's innocence had anything to do with his allowance of extra privileges. After all when these letters had been written their authors had not known they would be intercepted. The letters from Peter curiously lent to his feeling of, what Anthony called back bone. It was clear from every turn of the prose that Peter wanted the truth, and while he may have been privy to some parts of the police enquiry, even he didn't know what had actually transpired. The long and the short of it was that Anthony may have felt like the world hung slightly better for him than it had done previously, a problem shared and all.

The staff had also indicated that he may be in a position to correspond in the other direction, that he could write home, and although his out going mail would also be read, he was keen to do this.

It perhaps should be some matter of note that David had not written. When Anthony had first received his mail he had gone through it quickly just to see if there was anything from

David, there was not. Initially he had hoped that David would have written also exonerating both himself and Anthony; it was amazing how David, Anthony's best friend, had been immediately discounted from any involvement. It he didn't know better Anthony would have thought this was a stitch up. However thinking through things it was probably better that David had not written, again he would not have known that Anthony's mail would be intercepted, and could have implemented the both of them the further. Once again Anthony had a firm resolve to hold his peace, he would not implicate either of them.

A couple of days later Elaine accosted him as she was coming out of the office, she handed him a brown envelope. "It was a very close thing," she said. "I can't see that it will be the same next time but we'll have to wait and see."
As Anthony took the envelope he thanked her, and wandering along the corridor towards the day room he opened it. On a piece of paper far too large for its message, was a simple one line statement that his application for parole had been denied. He would have to wait another eighteen months to two years before he could make another. For all the good his mother's letters had done in raising his spirits he felt very gloomy.

Now was a time Anthony needed to think, he needed to do that more than anything. But what with the drugs he was being plied with his head felt like a piece of wood. Try as he may he could not get it into gear, it was with this background that he woke up one morning to find there was a terrific panic going on. One of the older inmates that had been on the ward longer than anyone cared to remember had gone missing. Nurses were busying themselves here and there, room searches and strip searches were being organised. Outside policemen were combing the surrounding areas and the inmates were almost triumphant that someone had at last escaped. As Anthony entered the day room someone was whistling the theme tune to the film the Great Escape, much as the staff found that highly disrespectful there was actually nothing they could do about it other than ask tacitly whether he could keep it down.

Anthony Johnson

It was not until the afternoon that there was some resolution to the events that had transpired. It went round in a whisper, how it was leaked to the inmates perhaps it would do better not to ask, but they knew. Wally one of the oldest people on the ward had not escaped, not in the sense that he had made a run for it. He was dead.

Quite how he had been able to get through the system of locked doors was something the staff would probably never resolve.

What was well documented however was that he had suffered from depression for a very long time. Depression, that is not a word that means you are just having a bad day or that you have just split up from your boyfriend. It is a word that describes a clinical condition. Sufferers of depression speak of an immense void, a huge black dark empty space where nothing will permeate that overwhelming sense of despair. A feeling of such intensity that it will annihilate every last vestige of hope.

Following the demise of Wally there was, naturally enough, a review of security and generally it was stepped up. As far as the inmates were concerned the delight they had shared in Wally's escape soon turned to despondency and everybody felt that little bit more isolated, that little bit more lonely. Because Anthony had been so keen to spend his time doing something, anything really, he was escorted once a week down to the Occupational Therapy Unit where he sat in on a pottery class. True enough a member of staff, singled out for that duty in itself, sat just round the corner having a cup of tea, while Anthony dutifully got on with whatever he was supposed to be doing. This group was not only a mixed group but it included clients from other wards. While Anthony had been keen to dispel any feelings of animosity based on the knowledge that he was attending the secure unit, he found in general the other members of the class were both friendly and helpful. At the outset he found it difficult to make easy conversation, his mind was so stuffed up with thoughts about how he had arrived there, but he soon found one or two of the others were happy enough to make small talk regardless.

As I have suggested Anthony was not someone that found it difficult to do things with his hands. At various stages of his life he had been involved with painting and woodwork and so he did not find it particularly difficult to apply himself to the making of pots. There was an in joke that kind of passed him by, that the first pot one made was always an ashtray. What he would have liked to have been able to do though was to fashion a figurine, not like those of Royal Doulton, no, he would have liked to make a military figure. Although for the first few weeks he found himself embroiled with the making of coil pots, and what he lacked in skill he certainly made up for in patience. However he continually made note of the staffing levels and general security. Two whole years, surely that was too long to wait, before he would be up for parole again. At some point he was going to have to make his move.

Anthony had imagined, somewhat romantically, that he would secret himself away and make notes on the coming and going of the various staff. From the outset it was going to be a game of cat and mouse, he would use his watch to time their arrivals and departures. He could imagine he as a prisoner planning the great escape, but within a week he had totally lost interest in the whole idea. The inescapable fact of the matter was that if he was to make a bid for his freedom it would in all probability involve the use of violence. What could not happen was for him to make a botched job. If he failed then he would obviously damage any hopes of early parole. It was with this back drop that Anthony decided to put the matter out of his mind for now, if he was to try and get free it would have to wait. The other problem that confounded any escape bid, was just where should he head, should he manage to get beyond the hospital gates. Eventually his will broke and he explained the whole sorry saga to Elaine in one of his therapy sessions. This in fact was a lot easier than one would at first expect, if he could he liked to try and keep these sessions to things that had happened around him, rather than go on long foraging missions into the past. Elaine herself had noticed this and after consultation with her own one-to-one decided that delving into Anthony's childhood would not necessarily be the best way forward. Whatever else transpired she had become acutely aware of how Anthony's mood could change on an hourly if not daily basis. So when he told her of how he had been looking to make an escape bid he was almost in tears, as he said it was not that the staff and everybody else did not treat him well, far from it. It was just that he could not imagine how he could last on the ward for another eighteen months, and that with no guarantee of his release even then. Behind the scenes there was genuine concern that he might be breaking up, the constant daily routine of being watched in every activity at every moment, the total lack of any privacy, the fear, all these could do strange things to a man's psyche.

His initial ardour for the affections of nurse Knightley were now beginning to wane. It was still the case that he could visualise her both in and out of uniform, but with the offer of what seemed to be a more mature friendship he found his thoughts taking him back to Lucy and Emily. In a sense they left less to the imagination after all he had seen both of these two women in the nude and as he had done when he was painting he could readily call either one to mind. But then on the other hand that was part of the charm of Elaine Knightley, one was never quite sure what was under that taut uniform. However diminished his affections may have been the thought of finding out would still occupy a good part of his fantasies. The very thought of stockings versus tights would console his troubled mind as he fell off to sleep.

Strangely, as he himself saw it, he found himself thinking more and more about Emily. Yes, she had been his first real love, but that in itself did not seem to be the rub. He wondered if he had been unkind to Emily, in all probability he had. He could remember swearing at her and drinking far too much, but that aside he had loved her, she wasn't just some sexual plaything. The very thought cut him to the quick. He could remember the large bosom and her fleshy rounded curves, but she was not fat. Built for comfort not for speed, but not in an ungainly manner. Curiously he found himself thinking about her feet. In any person there is very often a part that one just cannot remember, or a piece of clothing they wear regularly that one just can't call to mind.

For Anthony it was Emily's bra, he could see her bosom but he couldn't picture how it was supported., yet he knew she had worn one. On a scrap of paper that he had borrowed from the office and a pencil that he had also been loaned, he found that his doodling soon led him to draw a figure, it was undoubtedly that of Emily. Had he done the rightful thing and married her he could of spent a life time painting and admiring that curvaceous, voluptuous, delightful expanse that was her love.

However to say he spent all his time thinking about Emily would be untrue, there was also Lucy that took up a considerable amount of his time. Just as he had wondered had he really been fair to Emily, he now came to doubt Lucy's motives. At the time he had thought her the best thing since sliced bread, now he wondered whether she had been more fickle than he had been able to see at the time. He wondered had it been her that had made the going, certainly her disappearance had been uncanny.

In the way that some of us do sometimes Anthony had pigeon holed both women. Emily was larger, busty and had a warm personality and a generous nature. Lucy was slim and supple and was of an intellectual nature. It was true looking back on it, it had all been fun. And then Elaine, well that was different, he was not having a sexual relationship with Elaine, however much he perhaps wanted one. Unlike Anthony's parents who had met when his mother was nursing his father. In mental health there was a form of protocol that meant that at no point was there to be any form of fraternisation between nurses and patients, although as Anthony would have loved to observe, rules are only there to be broken. But as yet there did not seem any way that he could put that to nurse Knightley, who could say what would happen if he did? And it was things like this that gave him the resolve to remain on the ward and to attempt to work industriously towards his release. However long that took.

Anthony had at times that dubious quality of appearing the perfect gentleman, so much so that behind his back young women would refer to him being almost virginal. He might come and stay the night at the girl friends parents house and because it was the parents house would be on best behaviour only for them to say after he had left a perfect gentleman, but a wimp, or so he thought.

What had originally been a one off, an attempt to coax him out of himself, now became a monthly excursion to the staff canteen. And while his fellow inmates nudged and winked that he was well in there, Anthony took up his perfect gentleman act. He would not have a word said against Elaine and became quite cross should they make any form of sexual innuendo. "What got no balls?" One of them put to him. By rights he should have taken a swing at him, that was provocation enough, but he just grinned broadly, he was not going to jeopardize his position for the sake of some two bit insult.

"You know people are beginning to talk," said Elaine as she sipped her Sunday morning coffee.
"Let them," said Anthony curtly.
"Well that's all very well for you to say, its not your career that is on the line."
"I would have thought the powers that be," and with that he pointed upstairs. "Would have known that nothing has been going on."
"You mean God?"
"No the management."
"Only you pointed upwards."
"Don't the management live on the second floor." Anthony had her at a disadvantage.
"No, its just that you've come from church," she said.
"To be quite honest," he lied. "I'm not really sure I believe in all that."
"Oh," she said and a silence passed between them. Whatever conversation she had envisaged having with him had some how been lost.

"It may sound silly," she said, after a break in the conversation. "But you're not busy this afternoon?"
Anthony was tempted to say something very sarcastic but in the end he acquiesced. He was not busy that afternoon, at least not if anyone had a better idea of what to spend his time doing. The outcome of this somewhat fragmented

dialogue was that Elaine had wanted to invite him back to her residence. I say residence, not meaning it grandiosely, because she did not live in the nurse's home, she rented a two up two down within the grounds, a terrace house.

"I don't know why you have brought me here?" Anthony said, as Elaine turned the lock in the front door of her home. Later Anthony thought to himself that he had only really said that for want of something better to say. It had been a sign of nervousness.
"Oh, I just thought you might have liked to have seen how I live," she replied lightly.
"You don't consider it a violation of your privacy then?"
"Quite contrary. I wouldn't ask you if I felt that was the case. Here let me take your coat." With that Anthony took off his coat and handed it to her. As he went from the hall way to the lounge, he was pleasantly surprised to find that from the inside the place seemed larger than it had from the outside. There was the statutory three piece suite, that was if anything a tiny bit larger than was appropriate and the curtains looked as if they were made to match the wallpaper. The carpet was a thick wollen weave that gave the sensation that one was walking on something that was probably rather expensive, and although there was a relatively small television in the corner of the room, there was still that suggestion that it was fairly frequently watched.

"Sit yourself down. I'll make us some tea." And then after a pause, "Or perhaps you would prefer coffee."
"No tea will be just fine," Anthony replied in a voice that betrayed his false sense of security. "I think it is going to be difficult to find something to talk about that isn't work," Anthony continued. Elaine had been in the kitchen but now when she came in with the tea, she said, "Oh, I don't think so. There is plenty I don't know about you." She put the tray down on a smoked glass coffee table and began pouring the tea.

"Yes you've told me about your attempts at setting yourself up in business, but you've never really told me that much about your hobbies, what you like to do at weekends and the like. For that matter I don't really know if you like music and

then if you do, well, whose. For my part I may be able to shed a little light on what is going on behind the scenes."
"You wouldn't shine a light on your own personal life, I suppose," Anthony said this with an underlying current of anger, which Elaine promptly ignored.
"Well if it becomes appropriate perhaps. Now then let me see, I think I've heard you mention in passing that you once owned a metal detector."

It was in just these few sentences that the mood of the conversation was set and from it they did not depart and it was not until nearly half past four that Elaine agreed to walk Anthony back to the ward. For his part he was exhausted from talking so much, on hers she wondered whether she had done enough to foster some renewed form of relationship with him.

Elaine had worked Saturday and even the couple of hours she had spent with Anthony were deductible, so she wasn't due to be on the ward until the Tuesday. The fact that she did not run a car had been in her favour when she had applied for her house on the campus. However it also meant that she was forced into using the staff transport if she wanted to go into town and on this Monday she did. She was going to spoil herself and do a bit of shopping, Monday was a particularly good day for this as there would be relatively few people about. So it was not until the Tuesday that she saw that Vicky Chandler the ward psychologist had pencilled in for the two of them to meet. Vicky had neither the position or the nature to rebuke Elaine and in all probability it was that she felt she should just make herself available should Elaine need it.

"I'll come right out with it," said Vicky, after the two of them had sat down. "Are you in love with Anthony Johnson?"
There was a short pause while the red of Elaine's face slowly died and a broad smile took over.
"You are kidding I take it?"
"Well that is for you to know, but it does concern me that it wouldn't be impossible for Anthony to get the wrong end of the stick."
"Is that what has as been saying?"

"No, but then it is his reluctance to say anything about your meetings that is in part my worry."

"Look," said Elaine, now clearly on the defensive. "I just took him out, with the backing of yourself, to offer him some form of treat after you and one or two others suggested that he was perhaps unlikely to be as guilty as we first thought. What is it? You are going to go back on that now?" For all the world she was angry enough to walk out of that room right now.

"Look no one is saying that, but you must have noticed Anthony has taken something of a shine to you."

"Is that wrong, he is a normal heterosexual male, deprived of any genuine intercourse. I think if I was in his position I'd fantasize."

"But you don't?"

"Quite frankly," said Elaine still with her feathers very ruffled. "I don't see that as any of your business." Now that her temper was cooling she began wondering whether she would have done better to have walked out. "Let me ask you? You've never fancied someone on the ward? Perhaps a male nurse whose happily married or a client that happens to be particularly good looking. No, you tell me you haven't."

Now it was the turn of Vicky to feel indignant and she began to wish she had never initiated the conversation and their meeting. She had proposed speaking with Elaine before the consultant felt it necessary to stick his oar in, now she couldn't have cared a damn. That was not good.

The fact that Elaine and Vicky were more than just colleagues they were the very best of friends meant that neither of them would harbour any long term grudge against the other. But as much as Vicky wanted to make sure nothing untoward happened to her friend, Elaine for her part felt that Vicky was doubtful of her professional ability. Years later they would both look back upon the events of recent times and have a laugh. It is both beautiful and a little unusual that events having moved into the past become funny or embarrassing, directly in proportion to their importance at the time. It was then tempting for Elaine to take out her frustration against Anthony and only by consultation did she find it in her heart to befriend him once again.

As surely as time marches on Anthony's stay at the secure wing eventually came to an end and although there was no marked celebration Anthony found himself well pleased at being transferred to one of the ordinary wards. While he was still on section the first real sign of his new found independence was that within a few months he was granted leave to visit his mother at home, although it would fall to Peter to pick him up.

And it is here that I am afraid we are going to have to leave Anthony. Suffice it to say the worst for him was now over and had he ever come clean about the nature of his involvement in the death of Thomas Mann it would have led to a situation both far more unbearable than he would have ever imagined. That is not to say however that he had not suffered, but thoughts about his so-called friend David left a bitter taste in his mouth.

Martin Williams

Banks and Greenbalme.

The day had just passed when, it being the twenty-first birthday of Mr. Banks, Mr. Greenbalme had passed over a not inconsiderable part of his estate to the former. Mr. Banks, Mr. Greenbalme's nephew, had known from a young age the favourability of this genuine act of generosity and that it would make him, in all worldly terms, very wealthy. Mr. Banks however did not take Mr. Greenbalme's name, as it had been through the latter's sister that Mr. Banks had come into the world. Both that sister and her spouse being generally of on unwelcome disposition, Harold Banks had found himself an orphan before eight of his years had passed and it had fallen thus to his uncle to do the right and proper thing and take him in.

Whether he would have realised his part of the estate had his uncle failed to take him in at that young age, seems unlikely. Certainly Mr. Greenbalme, having taken an admirable interest in the female of the species, had remained never-the-less a confirmed bachelor. It was not for the lack of wealth that he had been unable to find himself a suitable partner. But when his sister died he had all too willingly taken on the education and development of her son. It was not, as perhaps one might have thought, only due to his quite genuine feelings of remorse for the family and his orphaned nephew that he intervened. For at that time, like a lot of men who come into great amounts of wealth, he had become somewhat reclusive. Should he have been unaccustomed, with the frequency of ones visits (such as the few staff he retained) then it would have been without good reason that one was likely to find oneself unwelcome.

To give some idea of the extent of Mr. Greenbalme's wealth we must imagine, if we may, a main house, in its' accompanied garden, of seventy rooms or more. Further these rooms were so lavishly appointed it would be with a gasp that one realised the true extent of Arthur's monies. It was inconceivable then that Harold had grown up in a house no bigger than a communal work man's cottage and how Mr. Greenbalme had neglected to do anything to bring either his sister or her spawn into more favourable circumstances.

In short Mr. Greenbalme had hated Mr. Banks senior, Harold's father, with all the venom of a most poisonous viper. How strange then that now he would do so much for their son. On their deaths, first the husband's and then his wife, Mr. Greenbalme was not the least bit apologetic and it was said that he would have readily danced on either's grave. Even now when they were so long gone he would not hear mention of their name in his house. Harold, Mr. Banks the younger, was under no allusions as to the relationship suffered by his parents with Arthur. Arthur had failed to attend either funeral and it was only after Harold had resigned himself to going to the poor house that his uncle stepped in. It seemed that the sins of the father were not to be transferred to those of the son, not if Arthur had anything to do with it.

The part of the estate that was to be made over to Harold consisted largely of some rooms in the South Wing and a lesser number in the West. In all this meant some thirty rooms, so it was for the first time, should Harold feel the need, he could have complete independence. The vegetable, herb and flower gardens that adjoined the South Wing of the house were not to become Harold's. However at some considerable distance and buttressing up against the landscape garden there were a collection of farm buildings, wherein there was a dairy, a piggery and in adjacent fields that were left to pasture some sheep grazed. These lands were also to become Harold's.

Of course no inventory would be complete without the mention of the stables and the dogs that were kept and whilst Mr. Greenbalme was not without feeling of adversity towards hunting, it belied any country gentleman to be without Horse and Hounds.

I have brought it to the reader's attention that Mr. Greenbalme had a tendency towards reclusivity and so it was that for most of his years that the larger part of the house had remained locked up. That is to say there were dust sheets over the furniture and curtains and blinds kept the light of day from these rooms. The necessity of a large staff was then also superfluous and whilst Mr. Greenbalme was known to the local community he in fact played very little part in it. Do not get me wrong he, was not unliked in the neighbouring villages and outlying communities. However had the gardens and the farming upon the estate failed to provide a not insubstantial number of locals with a steady occupation, then perhaps he might not have been as popular as he was. In truth he took little interest in the gardens or the farm and having appointed a competent steward for the farm and a chief gardener, he allowed everything to carry on pretty much as they always had.

For all this he was not a snob and would be the first to supply a flagon of cider when the haymaking was done.

It could be said with all honesty, that Mr. Greenbalme was a self made man. He had made his money in shipping and having nursed his desire to own a veritable fleet of Merchant ships, had eventually sold the whole business lock stock and barrel for an absolute fortune. It was then that he had come down to this part of the country to embark on developing and maintaining what he now affectionately called the Greenbalme estate.

Although making ones money in trade may have seemed to the order of the day a little vulgar, Mr. Greenbalme had few reservations about joining the polite society that held such opinions. He was far more likely to take the attitude that money was that. Money, and as such held few secrets.

Whilst he, Arthur, had had a number of seemingly favourable relations with the opposite sex, at one point going as far as to contemplate marriage, sadly since he had taken on the estate he found himself less interested than he had been, for whatever reasons. Indeed in the climate of the day it was not beyond the realms of fantasy that he still might marry. However, in the parts of the outlying villages where gossip still abounded, it was generally agreed that Arthur had been jilted at the altar, thus making it difficult for him to form any new and strong attachment. In truth it was more likely than not that his sister's luckless entanglement had had the greater affect upon him. Certainly no one would have wished that for him, and even considering the prospect left him cold.

Arthur's sister, Jessica, as she was known, had married a certain T.E. Banks, Terence, and from that day on no word of mouth or letter of any kind was forth coming from Arthur.

It may be true that Arthur had made what money he had work for him, work very well indeed, but his parents had not been without some financial security. Whilst they were not enormously wealthy on a sort of Arthur's scale they were well to do. It should be understood then that both Jessica and Arthur were given all the benefits of a loving home and an admirable slice of education and it may further be said that as children Arthur and Jessica were inseparable.

In the years since Jessica's death, Arthur's attitude towards her had mellowed but little, and his vehement hatred of her former spouse seemed to endure regardless. However unlikely, Arthur, having made his fortune preferred to forgive the son, while he still felt an almost violent repudiation for all that concerned the boy's father.

It must be said though, that in fact Mr. Terence Banks was little more than a vagabond and a thief, the fact that he held such a terrifying hold over Jessica had only made Arthur hate him the more so. It may also be said that initially Jessica had been a reluctant newly wed and the poor soul had been forced into it only then to suffer a miscarriage. But in these days of at least outward austerity it may have been felt by some that she had brought that upon herself. So married she was.

It may be true that had Terence been able to put his drinking aside, which often exceeded what is generally known as excess, that he might perhaps have been able to make something of his life. In truth we are only scratching at the surface of Arthur Greenbalme's disgust and dislike for the pair of them. It went much deeper.

It was late in the day that Jessica had sent word to her

parents that she was running off with Mr. Banks in order to marry. That night the light went out in her father's eyes.

As her father sat turning the piece of paper that informed him of their daughter's wrong doing, over and over in his hands. Arthur could do no more than watch as the fire of the man's soul seemed slowly to extinguish. His mother had grabbed the note seeing the sense of despair like a dark cloud pass over her husband's brow. Now she too sat with her head buried in a handkerchief, gently but steadily sobbing.

Arthur had spent that day walking in the countryside and as soon as he entered the house it was clear something was very wrong. Though the fire was burning in the hearth the room was stony cold. It was as if that quintessential essence of life had in one blow completely evaporated. The blood around his father's frame had ceased to flow and the heart that pumped that blood was heavy with burden.

As in due course the note was passed to Arthur he was at first astounded but he then threw himself into an unprecedented and violent rage. In this rage he cursed her and from that day on they would never see each other again. Later however much Jessica's parents might entreat him he would not go back on his word. He had made a promise to himself and whatever else endured he would not write or set eyes upon her. Should she, Jessica, wish to contact Arthur her parents, their parents would make up some excuse but Jessica was only too sure of what the bottom line was and soon she did not bother.

One day, not that long in some respects after they had eloped, Arthur had made his way into the house unnoticed (don't get me wrong he wasn't trying to spy or anything). Unusually he had not called out to let them know he was arriving, but not for any particular reason. However he could then hear his parents talking from behind the scullery door.

"You know he beats her?" Which was said less as a question and more of a statement of fact. Mr. Greenbalme senior did not reply immediately, but then, without any

indication of emotion he said,
"Well it's her bed let her lie in it. Neither you or I did anything to promote this… this… this… marriage, if you can call it that. I am not to blame."
This was bravely said, for anyone that knew the man would know just how much he did blame himself. But it was said without any real emotion as if he was referring to someone in the distant past not his daughter who had run off with a vagabond.

"Don't you think there must be some way that we could help?" Again one could hear the desperation in the mother's voice but again the father reiterated that he had no part in it.

It was obvious that this conversation would continue in this manner for some time yet and Arthur did not feel it was in his interest to interrupt them. So without speaking to anyone and with his blood at almost boiling point, he made his way upstairs. His parents would continue, although now he would not be able to make out the individual words that were spoken and for their part, they only vaguely heard the noise on the stairs that in itself would not stop them.

He did not know with whom he was the more angry his sister or her spouse. It was easy to hate him, he had never loved him but that fact in itself seemed to make things worse not better. He could kill him. "It was her bed and she had made it," but for all that it did not really seem to redress the balance. He hated them both, for what they had done to him. Why yes. But what they had done to their parents was unforgivable. He would kneel and say a prayer but prayers are hard to come by when one feels such antipathy for the world and even harder to find if one feels justified in that.

Quite how the young Arthur was able to control his feelings is at first difficult to understand but to suffice it to say he took up a book and slowly started turning the pages. Focusing his mind in this fashion allowed him in part to overcome the worst of his frustrated anger.

This then is the background against which the adoption of Jessica's child is set. Thus it was when Harold thought about his life he would more often then not think about the time he had spent on the Greenbalme estate, dispensing with his life before that.

Memories of the ice cold bedrooms, where one was tempted to dive into bed fully dressed rather than run the chance of developing some dreaded lergy, brought on by those self same freezing rooms. For whilst Harold was to be made as comfortable as he could possibly hope for, his uncle had a strange belief that baring such hard ships were in themselves character building and hence no fire was ever lit in the boys bedroom.

But for all this Arthur was not seen as a hard task master. The young Harold during the summer months would enjoy playing in the gardens or visiting the stables if he should choose to wander further. He could go to the dairy or join in with the harvest. The fact that his education was in many respects somewhat privileged was in deed par for the course, although his uncle had left strict instructions with his tutor that on no account was his enthusiasm to be dented merely to prove a point of discipline. He felt that Harold's early experiences of the world were quite sufficiently demanding without future animosity to be held over him.

The long and the short of it was that he would not have the boy beaten.

When Harold looked further back into his life things were less defined than they were in more recent memories. He could remember his mother speaking of his father's death and for a boy that age he had wept very few tears concerning it all. He had imagined rightly or wrongly that that would make him head of the family, age six and three quarters. It was not then for him to go crying off. But then had his father been present when his mother had died, surely that was not quite right.

Naturally enough on the death of his mother he had been struck by an almost dangerous sense of morbidity and when his uncle had come to the rescue, he had failed miserably in showing the zeal and courage that he felt he ought. The fact that his uncle was not himself in fear of dying indeed took Harold some time to master. As indeed did his newly found circumstances and had he not been so bitterly tied up in the death of his nearest and dearest he would have looked upon his new home with awe.

When his father had died he had asked his mother how that had happened, no doubt hoping that for him a similar occurrence might be avoided. His mother had replied that he had died of intoxication and poverty. Was it then that his mother had died of the same? Well in that case his uncle and he were very well set to live a long time. His uncle obviously had plenty of money and perhaps only drank in moderation. The connection between his uncle and mother regarding the division of the estate did not even occur to Harold at this early age.

On his arrival at the Greenbalme estate Harold had practically no formal education to speak of and what little he did have were largely due to the efforts of his mother. It was not that he did not wish to attend school, he would have done so readily, but faced with a screaming mob of juniors who were only too pleased to relate to him how his mother was a whore and his father a drunk, playing truant seemed the more sensible thing to do. In short he was brutally bullied and that on top of his only too volatile home life, he soon found himself wandering the countryside. Making excursions for himself, coming home for no more than a meal and to rest, he was indomitably independent, and in part this made up for his lack of formal education.

Jessica, the boy's mother, would have gladly coached the lad herself and this could have made up some of the deficit but her day was a long hard one and for the most part spent doing other people's chores. This she did just to earn a few shillings to keep the boy clothed and fed.

His father was little help to the family's purse, either drinking what he earned or lounging round the house in a foul mood because he had not the money to do so, Jessica was often sick.

It seemed that from the moment Harold had entered the world Jessica had tried to instil in him some sense of worth or value. Thus she was prone to speak,
"You may not be the wealthiest of children, you may not be the happiest of children, you might have fallen on better circumstances, but rest assured there are worse off than you."
For the little Harold "worse off than you" seemed to reverbrate around his brain, like something that had got lost in a maze and had it not been for his uncle might have continued to do so for many a year hence. Though now he could look back on his mother's little anecdote with a wry smile, in her life time his current state of health and well being would have been unthinkable.

The very first time Harold set eyes on his uncle he realised immediately how wealthy he was, on seeing his new home he was almost struck dumb. His uncle had imagined, the boy being in mourning and all, that it would take a while before one could genuinely take up conversation with the young man. According to his uncle's wishes it was felt the boy should mourn the death of his mother and with that in mind a little black suit was supplied. In the course of time a veritable wardrobe of clothing became his, but it took a while before his fastidiousness in looking after them waned, thinking as he did that best clothes were worn on bank holidays and Sundays. Harold could still hear his mother scolding him for the wear and tear upon his clothes and as she had put it, "However did he think she would be able to supply new ones." Arthur however for his part did not intend to mourn and while he showed a modicum of respect for the boy's feelings he secretly damned his own.

Quickly Harold learned there was more to sitting at table than ever he had known in his previous existence. The food was plentiful and not to be bolted down like there was no tomorrow and should he want more, just the very thought of it! He was soon able to judge pretty well how things were going just by keeping an eye on his uncle over dinner. Whilst he was still a bit young to do so, he had noticed that Arthur would refer to his cellar and this was evidently something Arthur took great pride in.

Anthony Johnson

In the summer Harold would go down to the farm where the hay-making was in progress and he would play with the children of like age. Whilst the children of the farm labourers would think nothing of it, he could not help being somewhat aloof. Yes, he would willingly play with these children but he could not help but be the more aware that their future would be different from his.

How was it that they played hide and seek, he was so easily found? Perhaps he did not have the die hard resolve of those who had brothers and sisters to impress. His uncle, in his wisdom, had employed a tutor to teach the young Harold at home. This was partly out of sympathy for the boy's somewhat delicate predicament and partly because Arthur had a deep seated mistrust of the grandiose boarding schools. School that portended to give a "rounded education" to its pupils, while a blind eye was turned to the indomitable bullying that was seen as a matter of course.

Harold for his part enjoyed the education that he received and his instructor was quick to realise his potential. It would seem Harold had a particular flair for those things that might be called artistic in nature. He enjoyed composition and had an eye for detail that made him both a useful painter and a keen scientist. He soon progressed far beyond the standards that were normally set for a child of that age and without recourse to that great instrument of learning the horse whip.

As a point of fact Arthur, whom he now called uncle Arthur, made on the whole very few demands upon the boy's tutor. He expressed however and in keeping with the fashion of the day, that he felt a good grounding in Mathematics, Writing and Reading as well as a composite knowledge of the bible were the essentials of a good education. Further, that Music and a broad grounding in Art would, he felt, compliment more serious study in Latin, Greek, and languages. In short Harold's studies were to be pretty thorough and all that to a young man who had narrowly missed going the poor house.

In the summer months, when it was felt that his education

need not progress at the same rate, he could easily employ himself perhaps with a day's riding or an adventure down to the shallow pond and river where he could play with sticks or bathe. Although there was company to be had, in the form of the village lads, as often as not Harold preferred to keep his own. It was not that he disliked the company of the other boys, it was like or not that he just did not seek it out.

In truth Harold found it difficult to equate his newly found wealth and happiness with his former abject poverty. How could it be, that he had benefited so much from the death of his loved ones? It did indeed seem a very strange if not cruel judgement on life. Judgement... that was something he was going to have to think long and hard about. It would seem there was Biblical judgement and there was man's judgement, then there were the courts. He would not pass judgement upon his uncle, how could he when Arthur had shown him so much kindness.

Yet how was it that he had gained so much from such a loss. Quietly, secretly, Harold began forming in his mind an idea that perhaps one day he too would pass judgement. He would become a barrister and then a solicitor and then, with perhaps only the ease that children have the innocence to enjoy, he would become a judge. But for now to allow his thoughts to wander in such a manner, was a sure fire method of dealing with the inevitable deep rooted sense of melancholy that he harboured when he thought back to his parents predicament.

Now melancholy, there is a word that seems to preside over its' very sentiment with its' annunciation, and a word that would always carry Harold back to the side of his mother. But here we speak of melancholy not melancholia, a disease of the mind that could take a man to bed.

Although it was quite possible that Harold's mother had faced that very dilemma, it was then essential that Arthur do as much as he may to make sure that he did not fall foul of that self same presentment. And believing as he did that what one portrayed to the world at large, if even by proxy, effected the very core of ones own emotions, he determined to show only the better part of his nature. He was found to be at ease with a demonstration levity and frivolity, as he was afraid that he should be overtaken with a burdensome fit of melancholy. Thus it was that the defiant Arthur would laugh and joke with the very best of them regardless of whatever he felt inside and although it largely went unnoticed, his deeper darker fears remained with him and were not outwardly expressed in any way. The very hiding of them made him feel more at ease not less. Having said this, however, it seems that Harold's uncle was only too aware of the sadness in the boy and respecting of this would make allowances for the boy.

Certainly Arthur would have all too readily invited other boys to come to the house to play and pass the hours, but for the fact that Harold showed little or no interest in taking up this privilege. Strange as it must seem to us now, Harold was as happy as not with his own company and when Arthur enquired whether he would like boys to come from the village, he was like or not either disinterested or plainly negative.

Naturally it had occurred to Arthur that the boy could be sent away to some form of collegiate establishment, but being somewhat forward thinking for his day, Arthur frowned on an education system crowned by the use of the rod. He also frowned on the system of fagging and at the end of the day he did not really wish to part company with his newly found friend and companion. And whilst it was more universally agreed that such establishments turned out well mannered confident individuals, Arthur could not help but think that was in spite of the education they were given not because of it.

As has been noted here Arthur was and will always be a bachelor, the importance of this may become apparent, for Harold had not a mother. Arthur himself could not have been more aware of this had he tried and after a kind of probationary period when it would become clear which of his staff Harold felt the more comfortable with, it was decided that the former scullery maid should try in some respects to fill this void. Her name was Anne, she may have been a little older than the boy's own mother, she may have been a little younger. It had been during the boy's natural period of mourning that she had found favour with him and whilst the rest of the household scoffed, it had become apparent that during the boy's not infrequent visits to the kitchens, that she was a favourite. It was in this manner that she had sort of partly adopted the boy.

To describe Anne she was a stout, resolute woman, what one might have called in less austere circumstances, buxom. She cut an ample figure and this was if not complemented by a cheery round face and an healthy complexion. Her hair, which she often wore plaited, was a dark brown and if one stopped to think about it, she might have been a more likely figure to have seen down at the farm, perhaps milking the cows. And whilst that generous bosom and broad hips had failed to serve the purpose for which they had been meant, she took kindly to the idea that she should serve as a surrogate mother. But whilst Harold's uncle was as keenly aware of Harold's lack of parentage, and the need for them, Harold for his part did not in any manner conclude that they could replace the real thing. Such that while Arthur and Anne tried their damnedest to fill the void, Harold could no more accept that his friend and confidant his uncle, was anymore his parent, than the bouncy scullery maid, his mother. Over this he was never mistaken.

To add to his uncle's problems, as time progressed, Harold became more and more preoccupied with his former parent's situation. The fact that they were never to be spoken of only serving to fuel the burning desire the boy had to make an enquiry. Paradoxically as his enquiries increased so did the dark feelings of the inevitable powerlessness of his situation; to resolve what had become a family taboo. So it was that while so many of Harold's questions would remain unanswered there was seemingly nothing he could do to alleviate his curiosity.

Perhaps uppermost in Harold's mind was the incredible disparity between the social status of his late mother and father when compared with the affluence of his uncle. As the boy grew older it of course became more apparent to him that there must have been something seriously wrong for both brother and sister to live at such differing ends of the social strata. Indeed he would wonder whether Arthur had really any idea of the pain and deprivation that had been hurled upon his sister. Did Arthur have any comprehension of what it was like to endure a winter where there was for sustenance little more than a bowl full of gruel? And just the one, at some point during the day, and as often as not there was nothing. But beyond this Harold could not do otherwise than hold an enduring affection for his uncle. Had he not plucked Harold from the gates of the poor house? Had he not taken it upon himself to make Harold into a gentleman of sorts? Had his mother lived would he have yet the while ensconced the lad? All these and many others remained as questions that could not as yet be broached with his uncle. What was clear however was that in whatever way you looked upon it Harold was deeply indebted to his uncle.

As anyone may experience things as they find themselves disappearing more and more into the past become less poignant, so Arthur was as defiant as ever about allowing any discussion about his sister and brother in law, contrary to the general rule. However this was not the case in full and those around him that knew him best might just have discerned a softening of his approach. This was perhaps best portrayed by what he had thought was his silent mutterings out of earshot. To himself he would just whisper, "I'll be if the boy doesn't take his features from his mother." It is true of course that these mutterings in fact concerned the boy rather than his former family but in some respects even this may have been a step forward. But in his own mind he was as reluctant as ever to relinquish his lack of forgiveness in all that had been his sister's business. And it may be said that in as much as his features may have taken after his mother, in other respects he took after his grandfather. It became obvious that not only would he demonstrate a useful dose of athleticism, he looked to intents and purposes like he was going to turn out to be something of a giant. Had he been schooled in the manner necessary he could have presented the most enviable general on a battlefield, as it was he showed a placidity and emotional quality to him that had it ever been tested would have tried the patience of even the most prosaic Sargent Major's. Long before he came into that part of the grounds, outlying houses, and rooms of his own, villagers spoke of a man that was to be respected, both for his sense of reason and for his affection for those that worked around him. They felt that the day he did take over, the very last consideration on their minds was that he would be tyrannical, quite the contrary they looked forward to working under him. Not that they had ever had any cause for complaint under his uncle, although they felt the young man would bring changes. For where Arthur showed really very little interest in the general running of the estates, leaving it all to "his man", Harold in complete contrast would apply himself to just that with a fervour that did as well for the both of them if not more.

Harold would canter down to the outlying farmstead and involve himself as much with the mid summer harvest as he would with understanding the intricacies of animal husbandry, and what do you know, he had a flair for it. In the evenings he would sit down with his uncle and make, often in fairly general terms, comments and ideas, that perhaps his uncle's man could consider, meanwhile working in great detail behind the scenes. It had become apparent it would not be the Greenbalme estate forever, perhaps some day it would be the Banks estate.

I have spoken, if not perhaps a little turgidly, about the paths of both Harold and his uncle and concerning what, in the main could not, as well as that that may be referred to as a subject of conversation. The most obvious course being that no-one was to refer to Harold's parents or indeed any matters concerning his life before he came to the estate of his uncle. There was however a matter that was almost daily debated and whilst Arthur found the matter peevish, Harold on the other hand could not help making light of it.

It of course was a field, yes, you may make light, but to Arthur had it been a matter of life and death it could not have been more serious. A field I hear you say again.

Imagine for a moment the long drive through the gates and up to the house and in front of the house a gravel yard where should guests be arriving they would alight form their carriages; this may seem a little academic, as there were rarely any visitors to the house that were not local folk. There immediately opposite the front of the house was the offending field.

Whilst it is true that every attempt had been made to shield the view from the house: a wall and then a fence and some trees that had been planted. These served only to draw the eye even more towards this veritable blot. Perhaps you find it difficult to imagine how any one field could detract so much form the picturesque settings of the Greenbalme estate. But the situation was further exasperated by the insistence of the farmer, who one imagined owned the land, on using it for arable purposes, and hence it was never green but a ruddy brown in colour. Harold could well make light of this but his esoteric sense of harmony was the lesser for it. Years ago Arthur had had it out with Jessop the farmer of the land, and by all reports offered him anything if he would just give up this piece of land, or at the very least allow it to pass to pasture. For all his efforts he had been unsuccessful and the conversation that he had had with Jessop had gone into the world of folklore.

So he says, your man, 'Lookie hear Mr. Jessop,' for he did not want to offend the man and did not know that we call him just Jessop. 'Lookie hear I wonder if we could find some suitable arrangement concerning your field that buttresses onto the front of my estate.' Well you wouldn't know it but that was enough to get old Jessop's back up. He was never one for lots of language and he don't take kindly with folk meddling in his affairs, particularly what he calls foreigners, folk that weren't born here. So he says to Mr. Greenbalme, 'Ay that is my field.' Because you would have thought owt else, that Jessop was an honest man. That being the case Mr. Greenbalme put it to him that he'd like to acquire the field. Well Jessop he fixed him with his eye an says,

"Them's for me taties," and with that he turned and left Mr. Greenbalme to find his own way out."

It was unusual at this point for the re-enlightenment

congregation of the Stag and Hounds to show their pleasure at the recounting of this tale with laughter. And while none of them really held any malice towards, what was often as not their employer, he could never become country folk as they were.

So it was with great urgency, a couple of weeks after Harold had come into his own, that Arthur requested that the two should speak.
"Do you know I have the devilish piece of information?"
"What's that?" replied the younger. And although they were meeting in a part of the house where they were unlikely to be overheard Arthur still felt it necessary to lower the tone of his voice and consequently so did Harold.
"Do you know that piece of land, Jessop's land, at the front, its not even Jessop's. You know Lucy of course, one of the kitchen maids, well her fiance had been drinking late, may I say very late, and Jessop was as drunk as a lord and he let it slip."
"No, that can't be so," replied Harold again.
"He was stood at the bar and he says the funniest thing about that bit of land is, that it ain't even mine. Then he looks a bit sheepish. It wasn't just for us to hear and on tell of it seemed so unlikely. Well..." said his uncle, raising his voice a little and allowing his chest to broaden. "I'd never of imagined it. You know I don't like to keep such things to myself but how could it be true? With that in mind I've contacted a solicitor in London and they are due to send someone down to discuss it all in the next few days."
With this Harold looked over his uncle's shoulder at some papers and his uncle pointed out that they were to expect a Miss Clifford, however unlikely that seemed.

Miss Clifford, or Letty as she was known to her friends, her being a Charlottte, had been due to arrive on the Thursday. However partly due to the difficulties that had been encompassed by the London stage on the passage to the West country and in part due to the somewhat cavalier attitude expressed by its drivers and general staff, it was a day late. This meant that Mr. Brown, Arthur's man, who had been dispatched with the view to meeting her with a horse and carriage, to take her the last part of her journey; had the unenviable task of finding himself a bed for the night so that he could fulfil his duty the following morning. The very idea that he should return to the estate and make out afresh the next morning did not even occur to him. He knew further more that despite the eagerness that awaited her arrival it was unlikely that Arthur and Harold would imagine any harm had come to her, such was the reliability of the London stage.

There were, as with any reasonably sized town, a profundity of accommodations from which one could choose. There were Taverns, Inns and Hotels, and lodgings solely for the purpose of men that were travelling on rather than staying: wayfaring men. Whilst Mr. Brown had frequented many of these establishments over the years. Visiting the town on market days or in his younger days running errands for his boss. He was not sufficiently well known to anyone as he would imagine that they would automatically know his face. So it was with some surprise that as leaned against the bar in the Post Office tavern the wife of the publican, screwing up her eyes to do so, said,
"Why it is Mr. Brown if I'm not very much mistaken?"
And with this statement she smiled broadly while Mr. Brown nodded his assurance that it was.
"Well we haven't seen you in here, it must be nigh on a twelve month or more."
Mr. Brown had been so surprised by this veritable show of familiarity that he could do little more than splutter some form of indifference and yet she still felt the need to go further.
"You've been well I take it? Well you always was a strong straight fellow and you don't look any worse for the wear."
At this point she grabbed her husband's arm, he was also serving in the bar.
"Don't ye remember our Mr. Brown worked up on Arthur Greenbalme's estate?"
The husband, if not a little unlike Mr. Brown, also nodded his ascent. He too would have been quite content to find a quiet part of the bar where he could sup his pint in peace.

The day itself had not been a particularly warm one and the cold, as any farmer will tell you, is an admirable opponent.

Mr. Brown made his excuses and returned to the hearth to warm himself by the fire side and with a long sigh took out his pipe and tobacco.

Mr. Brown sat looking into the fire, watching the flames lick the chimney breast and the embers fall into the grate. He mused quietly to himself, recalling with some pleasure how he had started as a stable boy at the tender age of fifteen. For Mr. Brown things had been very different then, he had not a care in the world. As his thoughts progressed chronologically through to the present day, he imagined how very different his life could have been had Mr. Greenbalme failed to seek him out as an estates manager. He would not have witnessed the development of that estate nor would he have held such a vital role in its accomplishments.

When he had been approached by Arthur it was such a monumental increase in position and wages, that he had initially thought someone was playing a rather unkind form of practical joke. But he had determined to stand his ground and play along, it was with a little chuckle that he recalled how he had nearly missed his biggest chance in life. There was no doubt however that Arthur had had his monies worth and albeit Mr. Brown had quickly found his feet, he had proved invaluable in matters too numerable to mention here. He was not only Arthur's right hand man, he was also friend, confidant and companion, and so it was with a significant degree of concentration that he brought his mind to bear on things current. He hadn't said anything to Arthur, after all he did not really have enough to go on. And yet in some ways he was a little concerned over the turn of events in recent weeks. Perhaps he could put it down to his country folk upbringing, but he couldn't help but think that there was something a foot. He did not like conspiracies and over this field of Jessop's there had certainly been one. He wouldn't go as far as to say there was an Omen, that was the silly prattle of country folk. Yet it could not be disputed that this revelation had come at an odd time, what with Harold coming into his own and all. Had Jessop let it go with more intent than those around him accredited him for, that was not impossible. He must have known with the information that the field was not owned by him but by another, he stood to lose it and yet he had been drunk as they come on many an occasion and had never let this information slip. Mr. Brown wondered whether it was with complete contempt that Jessop was showing who he considered to be in charge and it wasn't Arthur, but surely that could not be.

Ordering from the bar another pint and some vitals to go with it Mr. Brown decided to make some effort not to spend the whole evening considering this issue. Once again making himself comfortable in his seat by the fire he could not help but notice a couple playing cards at a nearby table. Not in all the world would he have joined them, but was quite content to watch as the run of the cards went first one way and then the other. He had not known it but he was more tired than he had thought and with the warmth of the fire his bed beckoned.

Mr. Brown, Jeremiah Brown, had never known who was responsible for recommending him to Arthur and, true to form, Arthur had never raised the matter for discussion. Initially Mr. Brown had avoided the matter concerned, as only a young person could, that it might somehow reflect on his willingness to carry out his employ. Then as time had been eroded he had convinced himself that to ask would be an impertinence. Now he simply had no reason really to know, for had he known he surely would have thanked that person in excess. It may be said that, yes, Mr. Brown on gaining Arthur's employ had made the very best of it. However there must have been a hundred and one other applicants with better or at least no worse qualifications than he and many with ample experience, something Mr. Brown must surely have been seen as lacking in. He knew a little of animal husbandry and a little of farming in general, but surely what was most against him was his age. In fact all these qualities, as perhaps they may be seen, had been explained in full to Arthur when the original recommendation had been made, it may be said further that it was the local pastor who had been so keen to recommend him. "An honest man," the pastor vouched, "and there's not so many of those now-a-days."

Arthur and the pastor had originally met in order to discuss a quite different matter. It was not until this other subject had been completely dealth with, that Arthur, finding the pastor himself an honest man, confided just how little he knew about the running of such an estate. Arthur had reservations about even entering into such a venture, and it was only after visiting the house and its surrounding lands that he slowly but surely began to fall in love with it. The house and its estates had originally belonged to a man called Chorley, who had no immediate family to take it on and who had run up such terrible debts as to require its sale in the earliest proximity. Arthur wanting, as he did, to enter into just that sort of transaction seemed the perfect customer. It was while Arthur had been going over the house, as he seemed to almost weekly, that the pastor from the neighbouring village called upon him.

"You will excuse the intrusion, I trust. But I just happened to be passing and had heard that a prospective buyer might be looking over the property and thought I'd just drop in."
Arthur had to try pretty hard but he did get a word in.
"Benjamin Grouse at your service. I'm the local pastor, but then you can see that for yourself."
He stuck out his hand in determination that it would be shaken.
"Mr. Chorley, the previous owner was, God rest his soul, not a God fearing man, but it does no good to speak ill of the dead. You follow the faith yourself, why of course its obvious you do, I can always spot a sinner, and you are no sinner."
Mr. Greenbalme was not sure at that precise moment whether he wished to be a Christian either.

"You know of course that there's a chapel in the house, fifteenth century or was it twelfth, not as I suppose anyone would worry. Mr. Chorley well he never practiced there nor anywhere else as far as anyone knows. Shall we say he was not a God fearing man."

As I have outlined Mr. Greenbalme was not a large man, but if it was possible the pastor was even smaller, with a shot of dark brown hair and a portly gait one could not on first meeting, imagine him doing anything but preaching the word of God. And while he professed to be within the realms of the C of E, one felt he had at least a strong bent towards the Quaker or perhaps the Plymouth brethren.

One then might imagine that a less likely friend and confidant to Arthur could not be found and yet curiously Arthur almost immediately took to him. Perhaps it was the loneliness of the position that Arthur found himself in, after all looking at property when one has no spouse in mind can be heart wrenching. It must also be said that the almost joyous, triumphal manner in which the pastor made himself welcome, was not rude as it might have been in any other employ, but spoke of some genuine concern. So it was that the pastor, Benjamin Grouse, and Mr. Greenbalme, from the most unlikely of introductions, found in each other the true measure of friendship and company.

The pastor was not by any means wealthy, in fact had one not known better, one would have imagined his faith forbade the amassing of any form of wealth but to Arthur his judgement was sacrosanct. Where Arthur had no knowledge of how the land lay, be it the hiring of workmen to put the house in order or putting out to tender for staff. Benjamin was with him and in addition the right hand man he had argued would be best fill the post of Estates Manager. When Harold had come to the house, Benjamin had been the first to pronounce Arthur as a genuinely charitable man.

So it was that Mr. Brown spent a quiet night in the Post Office Tavern, not unlike many country folk he was used to rising early. He had asked that breakfast be served at half past seven, but even at this hour he would have long finished his ablutions and had spent a considerable amount of time going over some papers and their relative figures. Breakfast served, which whilst ample, he took pleasure in polishing off, he settled his account and made off towards the stage and trap offices.
"Any sight of her yet?" The "her" that was referred to was not Miss Clifford but the stage itself.
"She'll be in twelve midday, I'm counting on it."
The little man that sat behind the counter in the Stage's offices, was a scrawny, lithe creature that should have been retired a decade ago.

If ever there was a stereo type for this sort of man, then surely this one fitted it to a tee. To say he was balding belies the fact that it was something that had happened a very long time ago and while a wisp of hair was drawn from one side of the head to the other, it did little to mask the fact. He wore half rimmed spectacles which slipped towards the end of his nose and wore the peak of a cap, without the rest of the cap. His dark trousers and waist coat, which were religiously worn without a jacket, did little to disguise the flamboyance of his rather loud striped shirt. All this aside perhaps his greatest attribute was that he could predict the arrival of the stage with almost stealth like accuracy and for this he was known throughout the county. So it was that Mr. Brown, standing on the opposite side of the street to the office, took out his fob watch to observe the time. And so with undue accord, as his watch presumed to declare that it was eleven fifty eight, the clattering of horses' hooves and with it all the calamity one could imagine, announced the arrival of the stage.

It appeared from nowhere, and set to allow the passengers to alight and while there had been only the two, a great display was made of making their luggage available. This may have been the greater case, both travellers being female and hence more luggage to dispose of .

Mr. Brown, in no doubt as to which of these two ladies was Miss Clifford, immediately stepped forth to introduce himself to the elder of the two women, the other being, at least in his eyes, young enough to be the formers daughter.
"Miss Clifford I presume. I trust you have had a reasonable passage."
It was obvious by the way she touched her hair and flushed a little that she felt she had been generously complimented and with a haughty indignant air proceeded towards the office. It was then that the younger of the two, lugging as she did a heavy suit case, approached Mr. Brown.
"Excuse me, sir, did I hear you ask for Miss Clifford?"
"You did indeed young lady." Angry at having made such an avoidable error he was a little terse.
"Well begging you pardon, sir, I am Miss Clifford."

"You are Miss Clifford?" he repeated. With an air that suggested he had not as yet quite got that on board. Now it was his turn to be somehow indignant and rather pompous. But then with a delightful quickness of mind and body he picked up her bags and dismissed the matter.
"Follow me young lady," and with that he whisked her off towards the stables where the horses had rested and his trap lay waiting. It was only afterwards, when he relayed the story to Arthur, he wished he had been kinder in allowing her to prepare for the second part of her journey.

It took no time at all for Mr. Brown to realise that Miss Clifford or Lotty as she insisted was no country lass and in that he was quite correct. Instead of sitting within the carriage as almost any woman that Mr. Brown knew would have relished, she immediately made it clear that she wanted to ride shot gun. But as a precaution against her appearing common he was to inform her when they were within spitting distance of the estate so that she could alight and take up a more composed manner in the trap. In a moment of bravado Mr. Brown suggested that she take up the reins but she was adamant that she neither had the talent or the knowledge to take up his request. In truth she felt comfortable next to Mr. Brown and would tug at his arm, as she pointed out this or that about the countryside. How the little houses were quaint, Mr. Brown could think of another word but he did not want to dispel the charity with which she looked upon his native lands.

In part because he needed to concentrate on what he was doing and in part because he had no natural flair in making small talk with the ladies, he was more or less generally quiet. However Lotty more than made up for his reluctance to converse and kept up a veritable barrage of conversation, that when he thought about it all seemed to merge into some nonsensical patter. In her quieter moments when she was perhaps involved in looking at a particular something in the distance, he amused himself, not without a chuckle, recalling how he had been mistaken back at the stage coach office. Further he did not dare to imagine what Harold and Mr. Greenbalme might make of her. Sure she was a spirited girl he would give her due for that. But what one could not possibly comprehend from this introduction was that she was delightfully attractive. Nay, I say, in some circles she might have been pretty. She had the looks if not the inclination to be a veritable man killer and Mr. Brown determined that he was not to allow himself to stare, still caught himself paying more attention to her profile than the road and his trap.

She wore a hat and indeed had brought with her amongst her luggage a hat box, so one presumes she had others. To Mr. Brown's untrained eye it spoke reams of London chic, for all he knew it could be the latest fashion. The country girls, if they wore hats, which might only be on a festival day or perhaps to church, generally wore straw hats. This hat was not of straw, far from it, it had been tailored. And her waist, as one had to admit it had probably been tied in with the very tightest of stays, but Mr. Brown had it in his mind that should he put his hands around her waist they would surely meet. But for all her attributes, her hair, her clothes, her shoes even her softly spoken up town accent, her face shone with a radiance that brought joy to the observer. I don't think I can explain how her features conspired with each other to produce such a generous measure of both quiet and beauty, but they did.

Charlotte's blonde ringlet curls fell about her rounded face; they were all the rage in London. She had a small mouth that seemed to pout sensuality and her eyes were dark whirlpools that took one on a journey right to her very core. But for all that she was as excitable as a newly born lamb playing in the dew of an early morning. Later Mr. Brown would explain how she had pulled at his sleeve every five or six miles of their journey and had eventually been set down so that she could arrive in style. With the wisdom that age brings both Arthur and Mr. Brown could not help but find this amusing but in an endearing kind of way for all that.

The clatter of horses' hooves and steel rimmed wheels announced her arrival and while Harold and Arthur had been sort of waiting, without knowledge of what was to come, they had not been that attentive to that end. As the carriage rolled up to the house the pair of them went out to greet their visitor.

As it may be she disembarked, Harold was stuck dumb. Veritably his eyes went out on stalks and his body froze to the spot. Observing this, as he could not fail to do so, Arthur took up the reins and helping her alight form the carriage asked in a pleasant enough manner, if her journey had been reasonable. A little affected himself I do believe, he went on to explain how they had in fact expected her a day earlier and was thus able to dispel any embarrassment on his or her part. Giving Harold a little frown, as if she was not quite sure what had happened in that quarter, she proceeded to babble away about her journey, the house, her errand and all at such a vociferous pace that hardly anyone had any idea of what she was saying. On the marble steps that led into the main hall, and whether as a method of courtesy to persons present or just out of sheer intrigue, she firstly looked over her shoulder and then turned round to observe the offending field. And whilst it should be said that in all probability it was something that wouldn't have particularly worried her she could never-the-less understand the annoyance felt by Mr. Greenbalme.

It may be that at this juncture it might be wise to add a little background concerning Miss Clifford. For make no mistake, whilst her uncle's intentions by sending for her, were not in themselves mercenary, she was definitely here through no accident.

Surprisingly, or so it may seem, Harold and Charlotte shared an almost vital mishap; they were both orphaned. For whilst Harold definitely would not have been here had that not been so, in some respects the same was true of Charlotte; there however the similarities largely end. For although Charlotte was under the care of her uncle she had spent most of her life to date away from home and her parents, while they were perhaps not inordinately wealthy, had been far from destitute. So it was that her uncle had acted largely as their executor rather than their replacement.

It may be said that in many respects Charlotte's life had been not unlike the mirror image of Harold's; everything had happened in reverse. Her uncle was a mean old stick who viewed Charlotte with the same amount of contempt that he usually reserved only for women; they were either frivolous or conniving, or both. Quite how Mr. Greenbalme had ever been introduced to him I'm not sure even he could remember. Suffice it to say that in legal matters he was more than proficient and yet he had been a little embarrassed himself when he realised that concerning this field he could himself appear wanting in the matter. Her parents in stark contrast had been delightful and when first one and then the other had succumbed to consumption it had been a nightmare of inconceivable proportions for our poor Charlotte. She had loved both parents dearly and when she was whisked off to boarding school, as the only appropriate place for her, she had imagined that in the due course of things she might possibly become a governess of some kind.

What with his view of women hence, one wonders what possible sense there can have been in his sending Lotty to deal with the Greenbalme matter. With his premise that women were basically useless what could he of meant by it? In truth one would very much like to be able to give him the benefit of the doubt and say that he had recanted. But one must suggest that in fact he wanted shot of Charlotte as soon as possible and that if he sent her on such a mission there was always the hope that she would be noticed. He did not really care whether it was a person of money who took her on or otherwise, but I suppose somewhere in his heart he hoped his sister's child would redeem herself.

I think as far as Arthur was concerned, he was struck by the maturity and practical common sense that this London based woman brought to their home. There was no disliking her and Arthur could not help but compare her with his own charge. Regardless of any true feeling she may have felt concerning the matter she did not speak down of her boss and she treated one and all with due respect. But just somewhere I believe Arthur may have seen a chink in her armour, she was not like the general run of country maidens that frequented the dairy or the fields when harvest was due. Yes, she was intelligent, becoming, even cute all these were attributes, but was she a little hard, he wasn't sure what it was. As for Harold he was veritably carried away, he could not help but praise her, be it in private or with company and a four day stay as she had outlined seemed almost cruel beside the depth of his feeling.

In true simplicity, the way Arthur was sometimes, he had arranged for her to have a room that overlooked the courtyard and hence the offending field, as if it was not sufficient to make his case he had to prove it also.

The maid that took Charlotte to her room was at pains to point out that she only had to ask and what ever it was she should be able to sort it out. While Charlotte was refreshing herself, the maid began the job of unpacking her, it soon became obvious that in sheer terms of dress Charlotte would more than exceed the expectations of her hosts.

"Shall I put out the black?" enquired the maid. "Or perhaps madam would prefer the blue?" She spoke of course of Charlotte's evening gowns. "And perhaps you might like a shawl, it's not always that warm as the evenings progress." Charlotte replied somewhat nonchalantly, "Whatever? But tell me?" she went on. "Are Mr. Brown and the others related in some way? For I can't make it out. Three fully grown men and not a woman among them?" It became obvious that whatever brief Charlotte had, it had not included details of whom she could most likely find to meet. This may seem improbable considering the somewhat mercenary nature with which her uncle had dispatched her, but it was none-the-less the case.

"Well some make the mistake that Mr. Brown would have been young Mr. Harold's uncle, and then some as think that Mr. Harold would have been Mr. Greenbalme's son. But that's not so not neither. In fact you would have to say, that Mr. Brown, well he's no relation at all, he's a hireling like myself. Didn't he say? But then I suppose he's a good deal more important being as he is Mr. Breenbalme's right hand man. Now Harold, his name is Banks, Mr. Banks I should say. He came to the estate as a young boy and is Arthur's, that is Mr. Greenbalme's, nephew, though they don't ever speak of it, as you'll probably gather. There now Miss does that make it plain for you?"

In truth, what with struggling with the maids broad West Country accent, and trying to concentrate on what she was saying, Lotty was as confused as when she had started. But she was at pains not to put the maid through the whole story again and smiled broadly.
"Now the black or the blue, Miss?" enquired the maid once again.
"Oh, I'll sort that out later. You may go."
Lotty sat on the edge of the bed her hands in front of her. She was aware just how far from home she was and it reminded her of her first days at boarding school and then she shook herself and made a mental note not to be so silly. Among her possessions she had a little book of poetry that she took with her everywhere and at times like these she would read a few stanzas to herself. She found fortitude in the little book. In part she was desperate to explore, in part she felt obliged to rejoin the others, in any event she found Mr. Greenbalme and his nephew in the library. It was obvious that both had been waiting for her to reappear. Between the two of them they had as many questions to put to her as she had for them. Perhaps the greatest of which was how Charlotte as such a junior, in age if not in position, found herself with them at the estate.

Charlotte and Harold, after their sojourn around the house, rejoined Arthur in the day room, which also served as the breakfast room. Charlotte was informed that dinner would be served at seven thirty and the maid informed her that seven thirty sharp was what was being recommended. Tired from her day's travelling, Charlotte retreated to the comfort of her room where she read for a while before getting ready for dinner. She had also been informed that Mr. Brown would be joining them, if only to make up the four.

As entrances go I believe this one would have held its ground with the best of them, but for mere country folk, such as Harold and Mr. Brown, it was astounding. She swept down the stairs in a blue silk evening dress, which was fitted in such a way, as to leave only a little to the imagination. It was low cut at the front and showed an almost indecent amount of flesh at the back. She looked and felt like a million dollars.

The four of them stood behind their respective chairs, Arthur was at the head of the table, with Mr. Brown sat at the opposite end. Which meant that Harold sat nearest to Charlotte each of them being at either side of the table. It would have been all too easy for Harold to spend the entire evening staring at Charlotte, so in order to compensate he endeavoured to eat the most part of the meal without looking up. And although he was not aware of it he still sent furtive looks in her direction.

A lull had dissolved in the conversation and I believe each party felt as embarrassed as the other that a form of impasse had been reached. Charlotte however showed her strong sense of independence and leaning forward to speak to Harold, she kicked him, and whispered, "Say something for God's sake."
Harold, who had been knocking back the wine like it had gone out of fashion, decided he'd propose a toast.
"To our friends present and our friends elsewhere."
Arthur, while joining in the toast, could not however do more than attempt to conceal his displeasure in this matter. But in light of the fact that conversation as yet still did not flow, he also proposed a toast.
"To our good friend Mr. Jessop, who unwittingly brought us all together."
And then from the other end of the table,
"I'll drink to that."
But Charlotte continued to press her case, she wanted to hear something albeit anything, from Harold. The fact that Harold was labouring under a somewhat alcoholic haze did nothing to change her mind in this matter.

She kicked him again. And then all of a sudden his mind was crystal clear. Whether it was that second kick in the shins or possibly the realisation that he was sat opposite an incredibly beautiful woman, who can say. But his brain tanked into gear.
"I wondered," he began. "I wondered, if perhaps Charlotte

and I would take a ride down to the farm tomorrow. After all I have showed her the interior of the estate. Is there any reason why I should not show the rest? And then as an after thought he added, "You do ride I take it, Miss Clifford." But this was more of an affirmation than a question, Harold naturally enough assuming everybody worth their sort would and could.

"Yes, that would be all right, I suppose. I haven't ridden in some years but I'm sure it will all come back to me." Then turning to Arthur, she asked, "How long have you been living on the estate here?"
It was obvious that she knew enough to know that Mr. Greenbalme had not inherited the lands, but one might forgive her for asking the question, whether it was genuine or not. Mr. Greenbalme answered her, but his nephew now had the bit between his teeth. "I myself of course was not born here on the estate. Mr. Greenbalme very kindly adopted me when I was still a young child."
It occurred to Charlotte that she could also tell a tale of woe concerning her parents, but declined to do so at this point.

The question that was on everybodys lips, but which not one of them as yet cared to enunciate, was how the devil did she manage to find employment with her uncle. The law in these days was almost an entirely male preserve and her uncle's view of women and their attributes or lack of them was fairly well known. But like the last page of a book when everything will be explained or so one hopes, not one of them had as yet asked.

Later when the meal had been finished and the gentlemen and indeed lady, withdrew to the library. Arthur managed just to catch his nephew unattended, Lotty was speaking with Mr. Brown.
"I hope your shins are sore enough? Whatever has got into you? You don't seem your usual self at all. I warn you be careful of this one, don't let her looks or airs and graces overtake you. She'll use you to get whatever she wants Mark my words, she's a city slicker and you can count on it, she'll view us down here as easy pickings."
Arthur had so much more he wanted to say, after all he had

hands on experience of working in the city. He'd seen silly girls marry into a fortune, he'd seen the demise of men whose wives made public their indiscretions, he'd seen men bankrupted trying to keep up the standards of living their flighty females required. And yet had he wanted he could have given Charlotte the benefit of the doubt, as it was he feared for the worst.

As Harold lay awake in his bed that night, he head clear, his senses alert, despite the amount of alcohol he had drunk. His mind went over the questions and answers that had been put to him during the day by Lotty. And then there she was in front of him, not literally, standing in her fantastic royal blue, low cut, evening dress. Then she was not even in that. She had inadvertently come down to dinner in her birthday suit and there she was stood in front of him, stark naked.

He woke realising that his dreams had concluded his thoughts, brought them to their rational conclusion and he noticed that he was hot and sweating. Instinctively he knew that he had that night's sleep and that he would not want for more until the following evening. That being the case he dressed himself and when he left the house the cool night air hit him again. It was a little cloudy overhead, but there was a breeze and Harold could not help but feel the cool night air mixed well with yesterday's alcohol.

He made his way through the walled garden, a garden that offered flowers for the house and herbs for the kitchen. He found himself in a large expanse of green grass and looked up to the sky. Between the myriad of clouds one could see the moon shining through and while it was by no means full, it still made a pretty sight. From there Harold moved towards the shelter of some trees, it had just started to spit and whilst the rain did not bother him, he again made for cover.

Thinking that he had heard something he stopped. Perhaps it had been a breaking twig or more likely something he had just imagined; he continued on his way. Then like a bear on a mountain side, right in front of him stood a man with a double barrelled shot gun, Harold was under no illusions as

to where it was being pointed.
"You just stay there, nice and steady, and we will see what we have got."
"It's me, Harold." He vaguely recognised the voice of the other.
"Gad sir, you gave me quite a fright," said the other standing his shot gun by his side. "Whatever made you come this way at this time of night?"
"I could very well ask you the same?" replied Harold.
"It's Nathan one of your uncle's ground men. I took you for a poacher. I didn't expect to find you here, at least not so far from the house."
Harold looked around him and decided he had come further than he had meant. Nathan made as if to go, but Harold called him back. He didn't have anything particular he wished to say, but for all the world he was as happy to pass the time of day with this stranger as any other. He lauded the healthy reality of this gentleman that worked his uncle's lands.

"Nathan," said Harold, out of the blue. "Do you believe in the devil?"
"Well," said Nathan. "Like as not, I go to church on a Sunday. An' they do say there is a heaven up above and that the fires of Hell are a burning down below us, but whether I sees Lucifer undoing the hand of God and all ye sinners cast down below. Well I'm not sure as I would like to say."
After a pause while both men seemed to think on this a little, Nathan again broke the silence.
"I'm not sure a young man like yourself should be concerned about him. Whatever made it come to mind?"
"Perhaps I shouldn't say, but my uncle said some very ungenerous things about a young visitor we have at the house. That then made me think, that wasn't very Christian."
"Forgive me if I'm wrong but I should think it would take a bit more than a few unchristian words to send your uncle's soul to the devil and from what I know of him he seems straight enough. I can't think he'd say anything, not without good reason."
Bidding Nathan farewell and trying to console the restless thoughts that were racing around his head, Harold set off

once again towards the main house. As he arrived at the stables, the nearest of the outlying buildings, the sky had begun to clear a little. The dark mauve of night had given itself up to a light blue heralding the advent of dawn. Entering the stables one or two of the horses brayed, welcoming the first visitor of the day. Although it was not usually his duty to do so never-the-less Harold knew what he was doing when he saddled one of the horses and led him outside to take him for an early morning ride.

So it was later that he arrived at the dairy, late enough in fact for the dairymaids to have started milking. From the height and stature of his horse he looked down upon them. They sat in the main on little three legged stools operating their own hands to squeeze the juice from the cow's udders. Over the years Harold had become acquainted with many of them, however there was also the transient work force that would appear like magic when the farm was at its busiest. "Hey lover boy!" Shouted one such member of staff. Those around her either giggled or kept their heads down obviously feeling some embarrassment.
"I hear you've got yourselves a proper lady staying at the house there. But don't you think you can forget your Lillian now mind. When she's long gone with her airs and graces there will still be that Lillian working away on your uncle's farm."

Although Harold blushed at what she was saying in fact she had shown considerable reserve, her usual way of speaking being much more towards the bawdy that that. Indeed one of the milking men, who for no apparent reason felt it was his job to give an opinion, was heard to say, "You keep him in check our Lillian."

It was generally agreed amongst these gentle country folk that at least for now Lillian was Harold's girl. Whilst neither he nor she had owned up to just how far things had gone. Lillian had only been teasing him with regard of any affection that was placed elsewhere. Indeed Harold the younger adolescent had imagined he had forsworn the farm manager to silence concerning the matter, failing as he did to understand that it was common knowledge not just throughout the farm, but also within the ale houses and outlying lands. But Arthur, having conferred with Mr. Brown, had decided not to tackle him on these rumours, he imagined it to be no more than a crush, a fancy or something similar. However it was an undisputed fact that over recent weeks Harold had strayed more towards the farm than he had done at any other time.

Heated as he had been, not even the return ride had been sufficient to calm his temper, he swanned into the breakfast room like he was ready to go ten rounds with the best of them.
"Not up yet?" He said in consternation, after the maid explained that they had not seen madam as yet. "Whatever time of day does she call this?"
"I expect, if I might be so bold, that she is recovering from her not inconsiderable journey of yesterday, Sir."
"Well, yes, I suppose so. But it is half past seven and some." Then with just a hint of insight, "Do you think London folk might not rise as we do generally?"
"That I can't say. But I think we should leave her a little longer, to come down by herself. You can go on and have your breakfast Sir and I'll see to Madam a little later."

So it was that Lotty was woken from a deep and profound sleep, by a gentle knocking on her door. The maid had brought water from which she was to wash and insisted, against Lotty's better judgement, that she would help her to dress; it was a little after half past eight.

Looking at her pocket watch Lotty was obliged to think it early at least by London standards, and while office workers and the like might start at eight or so a lady might not dress until quite late into the morning.
"Don't worry," said the maid. "It is not so very late and there will still be breakfast to be had."
"They generally start at such an hour?" Suggested Lotty, if not a little peeved.
"Oh no, madam. The master's been up a good hour or more, they would not call this early by anyone's standing."
"So I am in fact late," exclaimed the exasperated Lotty, almost ready to stamp her foot. The fact that the maid was

fussing around her, in order to allow her to dress, pulling at this, that and the other thing, did little more than make certain of her bad temper. Had she wished to be dressed she would have brought her own maid, she eventually said in desperation.

As I think I may have already mentioned the Day room also served as the Breakfast room or was it the other way round. In any event it was here that Lotty joined Arthur and Harold; the breakfast things had not yet been cleared away, in deference to their visitor. Lotty ate heartily recalling her hunger of yesterday and unsure when the opportunity to do so might occur again. When Harold had classes to attend he would generally do so in the library, leaving Arthur to himself in the day room. But when classes were suspended the opposite would apply, in either case Arthur would spend the lion's share of the morning wading through the previous day's newspapers. They were sent down from London a day late. Today, however, both Arthur and Harold had been waiting in the day room for their charge to arrive. Harold made no or very little effort to disguise his impatience in waiting and had veritably worn a groove in the hall carpet. Arthur, having proved himself ineffective at calming him, took to his newspapers with scant regard for him or anyone else.

So it was that they were almost like father and son when Lotty addressed them both after her meal.
"If it's not too early or inconvenient, I propose that perhaps this morning we might look over some of the papers I have brought." It did not even enter her mind that this was a very forward introduction and might be considered impolite. But then as far as Harold was concerned he was too oblivious to anything that she said, to notice.
"Well when you are ready?" Arthur replied with a little guffaw, just to say that her attitude had not gone unnoticed, but also that he was not offended.

The breakfast things having by now been cleared, Lotty took from a leather satchel, that she had brought for the purpose, a couple of salient documents that she had previously prepared. Putting them in front of Arthur she further withdrew a larger collection of said papers and put them on the table in front of her.

It is not necessary here to divulge every last little detail of what those papers contained, the most important of which was perhaps the certificate of ownership on the part of one Thomas Evans. Thomas Evans that lived in some completely unpronounceable Welsh village, somewhere in the valleys of South Wales; anyway it sounded like bandit country.

Again being a little too plain for her own good, Lotty explained,
"Had of course my uncle known at an earlier date that you had wanted to purchase the, may one call it, offending field he may have been able to help you earlier. But he asked me to stress that should Mr. Evans, for whatever reason, decide that he definitely does not wish to sell, there is then in fact very little anyone can do. It's his shout."

"So, is what you are trying to tell me, that we should proceed in this matter with some delicacy?" Chipped in Arthur.
"Well frankly no," replied Charlotte. "It appears to me that Mr. Evans is probably not in a position to turn you down. He is not a wealthy land owner far from it. He has a cottage and a small holding in the valley where he lives, but we are not aware of any other holdings in the valley where he lives. Indeed we have not satisfactorily determined how he came to own the land opposite your main entrance, merely that he does. Again I feel that I must express my master's annoyance in this matter, had we known about it we could have dealt with it sooner."
"That is all very well," replied Harold, feeling a little hurt. "But it was this man's Jessop's very intransigence, that led us to believe him to be the owner. And since every overture we made towards him proved useless, there seemed nothing we could do."
Casting a frown in Harold's direction as if to say that was not very business like of him she continued,
"However, it must be said, that even though you are in a position where you could offer Mr. Evans two of three times the land's value, it is still not a foregone conclusion that he

will sell. That being the case it occurs to my patron that in the first instance it would not be wise to offer over the odds. For if this were accepted then your outlay will have been the greater, conversely should such an offer be refused, then Mr. Evans may be led to think that the land has specific value above that which we would normally expect for such pasture. It would then seem prudent to begin with a smaller bid that is in keeping with the lands current value, if that is refused then we shall have to think again."

In Arthur's mind this was all now crystal clear, Harold however was having some difficulty keeping up.
"I imagine," continued Charlotte, "That if need be a surveyor could be called to evaluate the said land. But myself I think this would serve very little purpose and from your descriptions of the land and its current arable use and now I have seen it myself, the sum of fifty pounds sterling has suggested itself."

Try as he may to continue to present a confident, relaxed outlook and prevent his body language from completely giving himself away, he leaned back in his chair and for a moment was quiet. Fifty pounds sterling he thought to himself, in his day that would have been enough to purchase an entire small holding, land and buildings intact. Or perhaps as he might have had it furnish a ship and this was just a first offer, obviously things had changed. Standing up and leaning over using his fingers to support his arms, he expressed a wish to close the meeting, if that was alright with the other two parties.
"For myself I would like to take coffee in the library, you are welcome to join me, but then I imagine you probably have business of your own to take care of." And with that Arthur left the room.

"Oh, I do hope I haven't offended him." Said Lotty, as Harold took her out of the house and into the courtyard.
"It's not your fault," he said, in order to placate her. "I sometimes think my uncle lives in a time gone by."
"But he is very good to you, or at least he has been, that could not appear more obvious."
"Yes, that may be so."

"I mean if we were in London it would be unthinkable that we should be allowed to consort without a chaperon of some sort. In that he is either very forwards thinking or simply forgetful."
Harold would at this point have loved to unburden himself of the unbecoming remarks his uncle had made concerning her, but this would have been a betrayal one step too far. Rightly or wrongly he imagined that his uncle could not see any likely hood of inappropriate behaviour either on his part or Lotty's, he was therefore being trusted, and that trust he would not abuse.

Whilst Lotty kept up a steady banter of conversation he had slowly guided her towards the stables, recalling as he did his remarks over dinner. But when they arrived at the stables Lotty had an admission to make, "I'm afraid I'm not terribly good with animals, particularly large ones."
Trying to be kind Harold suggested that she might just come in and see the horses if they worried her, there was no obligation to ride. Against her better interests Lotty consented but no sooner had she approached what seemed to be a perfectly docile beast she started sneezing profoundly and could not stop. Realising that she had been talked into the visit rather than it being of her own free volition Harold immediately took her back outside, where she continued to sneeze until he eventually brought her a glass of water. And through her sneezes she was heard to say, "I think it's the hay that does it, I'll be alright in a minute, please excuse me."

All this and more pushed Harold further in thinking of her as a lady. Whatever his uncle would say about her being a "dangerous" sort, Harold could no more believe it than if he had been told not to trust Mr. Brown or one or other of his uncle's men. After Lotty's sneezing fit she felt it her due to release Harold to whatever were his daily pursuits and consequentially relieved herself for the afternoon which she spent quietly musing in the enclosed garden, while Harold rode.

The three of them would reconvene for a little light tea late in the afternoon and while Arthur had spent the best part of the day going over the business proposition before him in his own mind, he at this point made no reference to it. Charlotte having spent the afternoon reading as she walked (a little book of poetry), felt it was her job to exclaim about the weather and the beautiful surroundings. Harold on his part had enjoyed a daring ride across country.

That evening, the second of Charlotte's visit, they were not joined at the table by Mr. Brown, whom for whatever reason was occupied elsewhere. Again after grace had been said there was not initially much to be said of the conversation. Whether it was because the two of them had dined so often together, that they did not feel the need to speak; it seemed they were happy enough with that. In any event it was Arthur, probably all too conscious that he did not want to appear rude, who began.
"Miss Charlotte, may I ask if you have an interest in music? As you can imagine living out here in the country any amusement that we should find, tends to be from our own resources."
"Are you asking if I play?"
"I believe that is what my uncle is inquiring."
"Well to be honest, while I enjoy an evening at the theatre just as much as anyone, even more so perhaps. I haven't a note in my head. And although I would love to report that I could sing or play the violin or some such instrument, I'm afraid I'm completely useless with notes."

There was a pause for a moment while each digested what she had said and saw to their food.
"For myself," piped up Arthur, initiating the conversation again. "As a younger man I was always very taken by the organ."
Charlotte looked in his direction and nodded, to indicate her interest in what he was saying.
"Of course one can find ones instrument in almost any village hall, and I had hoped Harold might find a similar interest, but I think he prefers the piano forte."
"Then you play?" Inquired Charlotte turning to address Harold.
"Well yes, I can turn a little on the piano, but if you were to know, it is really my preference to sing."

"I had wondered whether we might presume upon you to sing after dinner, if our guest is not too tired from the day's activities to enjoy it."
"No, no. I would be delighted to enjoy Harold's singing, if he cared to do so?"

So it was Harold stood up in front of the piano and sang in a deep tenor and no sooner had he started than Charlotte suddenly felt all full up. She could not help it, it was not like anything she remembered experiencing, she had tears in her eyes, which had she not wiped them away, would have surely rolled down her cheeks. But she was not sad, not really upset, she felt joy but the tears were rolling down her face. And yet it seemed Harold was oblivious of any audience, again and again he took the melody, at once soft and deep than courageous and defiant. Through her tears Charlotte applauded and then begged for more, she was in her element. All too soon the entertainment was over and she was invited to take a night cap before she took her leave.

Later she would be lying in bed, that last brandy upon her tummy, thinking to herself she could not possibly drift off to sleep and in contradiction of herself doing exactly that. It was a heavy deep sleep, it was luxuriant, it was recumbent, if she had dreams she was not aware of them. It was a new sleep, not that of the city or of dorms, a sleep, if one may say it, that was profound. And when she woke, hearing that little knocking on her room door, it was as if she had slept for years.

The maid inquired whether it was alright for her to enter and Charlotte did not have the heart to refuse her, regardless of her own wishes. She would have been perfectly able to manage by herself, hadn't she done so these past few years, and yet she could not refuse a kindness. There was also something very motherly about the maid, was it a motherly practicability, and although it was not something that Charlotte did not fail to recognise, she had been without it a very long time. Further Lotty felt she could in some way confide in the maid, it being in general terms a very male dominated household. And she would also ask her of details that perhaps the men of the house would not or could not be relied upon to answer. So a little friendship of sorts grew up between the two of them.

Lotty went down to the day room, to attend breakfast and found once again that breakfast had been held over, and although she would not normally have had time for such pleasantries, she could not help but be grateful, despite her lack of appetite. What she did require, and in copious quantities, was coffee, if not to wake herself up, then to balance the not inconsiderable amount of alcohol she had taken the previous day.

"I trust that you are well and have slept well also?"
"Thank you Sir," it was Arthur who had addressed her. Flushing a little she continued, "I think this country air is beginning to take effect."
"Yes, you either love it or hate it," continued Arthur. "Myself I find it bracing but not unwelcome. I hear the air in London now, is somewhat dubious, but that may just be rumour."
"Indeed you are quite correct, Sir. The air in London is at times unbearable."
Arthur had given up correcting her as to the title by which she referred to him, he had asked her to call him Arthur countless times, but without success.
"I thought we would reconvene in the Library towards elevenish if that's suitable for you? I imagine there is not that much more to do to finalise this bit of business, although of course you are as welcome in this house as your uncle. He has always been more than just a lawyer to me."

After the breakfast things had been cleared away, tablecloth and all, Lotty spread out the papers, copies of which she had given Arthur, in front of her. So she sat at the vast mahogany table puzzling over this or that. Unbeknown to her she was being observed.

Harold had positioned himself by the side of the open door in such a way that it would be highly unlikely that he would be noticed, but at the same he could see Charlotte only too clearly. He could see her digesting the papers in front of her. He could see as she frowned and drew a line along a group of words with her fingernail. He could see her, with her small mouth, pouting and puckering her lips. He could watch as her blonde ringlet curls fell about her face, framing her beauty. He could watch as her eyes darted over the papers in front of her. He thought to himself, she is not like anyone you have ever met before. It is more than beauty, it is sublimity, it is an intellect. She is ... complex.... chic. More than anything else he wanted to aspire to his greater power, this city sleek

She looked up, was she aware of him? He did not think so. She hadn't got up and gone to the door, but how would he feel if he was discovered, how would he feel if he was not?

At a little after eleven Charlotte made her entrance in the library, Arthur had spent the morning there, he felt he was now aware of the proceedings that would follow. Harold for his part had arrived shortly after Lotty making as if he had been very busy somewhere else.
"If you will allow me," began Arthur. "I understand that this piece of land, the bane of my very existence, is in fact owned by a Mr. Evans of some unpronounceable village in the South of Wales, not as I had formally imagined by Jessop, who works that land. Further from what you have said here Mr. Evans might be only too pleased with a reasonable offer for that land, in so much as he does not seem to be a man of any great wealth otherwise. Against my better judgement, however you suggest that I might offer a sum in the region of fifty pounds which to my mind seems a very great deal, but then perhaps you know something of land values that I do not."

Not to be caught out, Charlotte again referred Arthur to a document that suggested a surveyor's report could be filed, but also from what had already passed before, that this might considerably delay things and the outcome be of little difference. Arthur was going to say that any delay would be as nothing compared with the wait he had had for the last twelve years, before someone finally told him who the true owner of the land was. However he said no more than if it was fifty pounds, then who was he to argue and if it took that to secure the land well so be it.

"As you might imagine my uncle," continued Charlotte. "Has had recourse to indulge Mr. Evans in some correspondence, if to do no more than establish that he is the right and lawful owner of the land. He has stressed however that no offer has been made without your prior agreement and as yet Mr. Evans has not been formally approached in the matter of a sale."

"Well yes that all seems in order. But I would like to know how your uncle imagines that we may proceed from here?"

Taking it up again Lotty continued,

"My uncle believes very much on the hands on approach, indeed that is how I come to be visiting you. It had been suggested, subject to your approval, naturally enough, that rather than heading home for London I should make my way over to Wales and take up the matter with Mr. Evans in person."

Harold saw his chance, "Well I think we can do better than that! I propose that I should accompany you to Wales and then if there is any haggling to be done, I'll be there on site with you. What do you think of that!"

It was obvious from Lotty's manner that she was at first reluctant in her own way, but what was more obvious was that she could be talked round. If Mr. Greenbalme could spare him and he wasn't too busy, and if he'd behave.... Rather pleased with herself in fact, all the more because this had come from him, there had been no prompting from her. If it turned out to be a disaster she would have at least that to fall back on.

It was decided Harold and Lotty would make the journey together and if anyone objected they would have to do so privately. The following day the morrow Mr. Brown would escort Lotty and Harold to Bexford from where they would take the post carriage and arrive at Mr. Evans' sometime in the next couple of days. If all went well and it was difficult to see at this stage why it wouldn't Harold would return sometime in the middle of the following week.

The journey Charlotte and Harold were to take to South Wales began innocently enough; Mr. Brown taking them into Bexford where they were to meet the stage. The two of them sat in the back of the gig nattering with all the exuberance of a party going to the coast on a hot summers day.

To Harold's surprise and Lotty's obvious delight they found they were on their own when they joined the Bristol bound stage and Lotty soon started her campaign for Harold's heart.
"At St. Margret's," for that was the boarding school that Harold had understood her to have attended. "I had a bosom friend called Phylis. We had come through from the junior school and we went everywhere together and did everything together. We would play tricks on the teachers who were almost entirely female and of whom the larger proportion were also nuns. Looking back on it, in fact I think we probably gave the nuns a harder time than they deserved. But perhaps you can imagine the situation, with three hundred odd girls, cooped up in this boarding school with a lot of ageing nuns and as the girls became of age. Well yes you can imagine."
Not wanting to hog the limelight completely Charlotte sat back in her chair in such a way as to suggest she was not finished but she would like to hear something of Harold's background. Of course in many ways this was the first time Harold had been able to speak to her in complete confidence, no one was likely to hear and even if they did there was no reason to suspect they would ever know of Arthur his uncle.
"While I must admit I have not had the benefit of a school education like yourself and that the study I have done has been largely guided by my uncle and the governor he appointed. It would be unfair to say I felt my education lacked in any way. The friends with whom I grew up, being on the whole children from the homesteads in the area, have treated me well enough but unlike you I can't boast a bosom friend. This is not to say I have been lonely. I have not."

"Well loneliness is in its self is a funny thing. Like you I was a single child and like you orphaned and I believe it was only because my uncle did not want me under his feet, so as to speak, that he sent me off to boarding school. While Phylis and I were not lonely, we had each other and God knows how many other friends and acquaintances, looking back I think we missed the company of the male of the species. Indeed the only time we might ever see a man was either when we ran into the caretaker (not much of a catch there) or when we were allowed to go walking, perhaps on a Sunday afternoon. As for the nuns virtuous as they were, I think privately they did not assume we would naturally follow in their footsteps.

"It may have been the nun's resistance to explain anything about the facts of life and the fact that en masse, at any given time tens of young girls were entering puberty, that our greater interest was aroused. So it was that Phylis and I began making our own tour in any particular direction, that, while it did not encompass any of the farmsteads would like as not bring us into contact with Alex."

"And Alex was the sort of bloke that might just give you an inkling into what goes on between the sheets, in certain households." Harold was trying his best to be attentive to what Charlotte was saying and although his mind ranged over an endless stream of possibilities, he largely succeeded. Although he was a year or so older than Charlotte, it was thought even at this point of history that the female of the species usually developed the faster. He could recall how Arthur had caught him perusing a book of prints, paintings of nudes and had he had the presence of mind he could have easily passed such a book off as reference for his own art work. It had been at that point that Arthur had taken the lad to one side and in a gentle affectionate manner explained, not only what he needed to know but also that the boy's current interest was not untoward but quite usually the case. If he hadn't been interested in women that would have been more of a problem not less. However, despite Charlotte's candour in recalling her early experiences of maidenhood, Harold felt no obligation to follow suit.

"Yes, it began to be our habit to meet Alex near one of the stiles that we regularly visited on our country walk we took on Sunday. At first it seemed only too ordinary, but for the fact that we didn't know any other men. He would stand at the stile and some form of competition would begin over who blushed the more. He was of course the perfect gentleman but as the weeks and months went by he became our secret love. That is until one day Phylis asked him for a kiss, I was livid, but I tried very hard to stay composed. Afterwards I asked her why she had done that and didn't she know that I also loved Alex? Yes she did, she had said and why didn't she think I could do the same, but I was deeply hurt."

Again Harold expressed his interest in what she was saying. Though truth be told he was finding it hard to stay alert as this curriculum vitae of Charlotte's early sex education continued. At last she put a question to him directly,
"Do you expect to marry, Harold?"
"Well to be honest it's something that I haven't put a great deal of consideration to as yet. But yes in the general throw of things I can't see why not."

As one might imagine travel by the post stage was as arduous as it was difficult. I speak not of highway men, thieves and vagabonds that could turn any journey into a disaster but merely of the roads and the discomfort of the stage itself. The stage progressing as it did, sometimes over roads that were no more than country lanes, with their encumbant potholes and pits. The weary traveller found himself thrown about like a buoy bobbing upon the sea and all the while the horses kept up their urgent forward motion.

So it was, that Harold was mid sentence, Charlotte took the opportunity of a particularly heavy bump and sprang headlong across the carriage. To say Harold was forced into catching her would of course be wrong, he was delighted to and making an adjustment with his arms meant that Charlotte's face was no more than nine inches from his. He had a hand on one thigh and another comfortably placed around her back and had no illusions that this had happened purely by accident. As he looked into Charlotte's eyes they were soft almost weepy and the little curl of her lip appeared to invite some further intimacy. She smiled,
"You may kiss me if you like." Charlotte spoke with a little break in her voice and there was no doubting Harold's desire to do so. What little experience the pair of them had in such matters was more than made up for in resolve and passion. When the stage pulled up in order to change horses it took a

minute or two for the pair of them to realise they were stationary and it was a heady mixture of love and passion that the coach master witnessed when the two stepped down to refresh themselves.

To Harold it seemed like an age that he sat at a table in the inn waiting while Charlotte spruced herself up in the Ladies and no amount of cheese, wine or bread was going to make any difference. Eventually she returned still a little flushed but obviously refreshed. What should he say to a woman he had just spent the last twenty minutes loving? Thankfully, as ever, Charlotte's resourceful nature came again to the fore, she was not stumped for conversation. While Harold was determined to offer any refreshment she might require, Charlotte was completely unphased and prattled along as if they had known each other for years, not just a week or less. It occurred to Harold that although he was listening, even intently, the words as Lotty spoke them were not getting through, they were like the seed that fell upon the stony ground. Try as he did to concentrate harder he found he could do no more than pick out a few individual words and perhaps just the odd sentence as for the whole it really made very little sense.

The horses changed, the stage driver invited them to take up their positions again, next stop Bristol.

"I think the first thing we ought to do is check into an inn of some sort," said Harold on their arrival in Bristol. They had alighted from the carriage somewhere near the old horse market, it was gone six and I believe Harold was worried that gaining an accommodation could prove difficult. For a lady and a gent such as they were an Hotel would not have been out of the question, but Harold had a mind to preserve their anonymity. This having been said Bristol was a major port and the last thing either of them wanted was to be caught up with the sailors and the whoring that went with them.

They tried one place which ostensibly seemed to have vacancies and then another, but it was with a little despondency that they eventually found themselves at the Plume of Feathers. They once again inquired whether there were rooms and the landlord passed them onto his wife, who apparently dealt with such matters.

"Our Sal will sort you out I've no doubt," said the publican with a broad Bristolian accent.

"Now would it be the one room or the two?" Beamed Sal as she addressed Harold.

"Well I think it would be just the one, if that's satisfactory." And with this he turned and smiled broadly at Lotty, not wanting to put her in a position she felt uncomfortable with and yet hoping that she would be pleased to share his bed.

"You'd be married folks then would you?" Inquired Sal in an interested manner and making with her hands that that might depend a little on just how much the two of them were prepared to spend. "After all I don't want folk a thinking that I'd be keeping sinners under my roof."

"Oh I think you can rest assured on that account," replied Harold, with a lilt in his voice that was faintly mocking. After all he imagined there had been many a sinner who had graced the bar if not these upstairs rooms. He was sure that if his money was good then this slightly quirky woman would be as happy enough to take it.

"Only I charge by the person not the room. You get my drift?" And at this point she peered right into Harold's eyes. From behind him he took Charlotte's hand and in that second she had decided and took the two of them along a corridor and presented them with a double room.

"It'll be four and six a night and breakfast is at eight." With that she swept past them and did not reappear, except in the bar.

"I suppose that's a might expensive wouldn't you say?" These were Harold's first words.

"It's delightful," were Lotty's.

For it was spacious and beautifully appointed, the best room in the house if they had of known it. Certainly it would have faired well against any room in one of the cities better hotels. Lotty threw herself across the double bed she was in seventh heaven.

Recovering herself from her reverie Charlotte then wanted to know what they were going to do next.

Anthony Johnson

"I think a little supper may be in order," began Harold. "But I think if you don't mind we won't eat here. After all neither of us wants to sit through the odious glances of the landlord and his wife, even if they were kind enough to give us this room. We may have passed an eating house on the way over here, I had a look and it seemed a possible."

Before Harold could get any further there was a knock on the door, so he signalled with a finger to his lips for Charlotte to be quiet. In all events however it turned out to be no more than the landlord bringing up their bags. Largely due to the lateness of the hour and the fact that they were not going to some banquet evening, they did not change for dinner. But after sprucing themselves up from a jug of water that stood on a table near the dressing table, they made to go out.

Once in the restaurant Charlotte immediately proclaimed that she had no appetite at all, however half way through her soup, she suddenly became ravenous and following Harold's lead order Roast Duck with all the trimmings. As the day had progressed Charlotte who usually tended towards an attitude of devil may care, had begun to be a little worried about the speed that things were happening. She wondered if even at this late hour a pastor could be found, who could perhaps legitimize what now appeared to be a fait accompli. She thought of Phylis and her contretemps with Alex and dismissed the whole problem from her mind as easily as it had arrived.

Harold on his part gave the idea of marriage to Charlotte no sentience what so ever. It simply did not enter his mind. Whilst he was led to understand that women of a certain ilk would not easily give up their virtue, he could not for one minute see how that affected him. Further he took the somewhat cavalier attitude that if one didn't taste the goods how was one to know they were fresh. And that in a nutshell was the rub.

As Charlotte looked across the dinner table at Harold, for all the world she wanted him to love her. If he would just do that then she could pardon any number of transgressions and yet I think at the back of her mind she all ready knew that with him there would always be some price or concession involved in any love he showed. So it was she was pleased to take the cool night air again, as they walked hand in hand back to the Inn where they were staying. And while they were both tired from their days travelling the next few hours would provide copious evidence of who they really were.

Returning to the security of their room, they once again embraced and kissed passionately, but Charlotte broke away from him almost patting him on the shoulder. She went behind the screen that stood in one corner of the room and began undressing. She removed all but her most essential under clothes and then with a spring in her step made towards the bed. Once under the bed clothes she removed even these and dropped them out of the side of the bed, letting them fall to the floor. Harold wondered if this had been the drill in her school days, for him nudity held no such embarrassments. He tore off his clothes in an almost violent passion, in some respects reminiscent of the way in which he ate. They would both sleep naked as only lovers and poorer folk do. For all his haste in making to bed, once they were both there together Harold melted. He was not going to take her in a flood of passion, rather he lay there in the dark, thinking of her with a due measure of tenderness. For some minutes he lay there, flat on his back, listening to the noises of the city, that lay all around. How different this was to the nights spent listening to the sheep on uncle's estate?

A little frightened, but with that easing, with an obvious show of affection, Charlotte put out her hand and clenched his. They lay hand in hand, naked, loving. As this hand was accepted in a moment she would turn to him and press her body up against his. Her hands would travel over his body, it all came so naturally, he appeared deep in thought. On his part he too, wanted to stimulate her body, not just with his hands but with kisses. He wanted to run his tongue the length of her and again quite naturally she began making little baying noises. Finally he would break into her and for the first time in her life she would know love, she would know sex. And though it hurt a little and she would whimper, she knew herself, she wanted. It was all too brief, but had seemed like an eternity. Now he lay again on his back, quick to catch his breath, and she by his side pouring over him. They would talk, she knew that much, she knew what was spoken of in her poetry book, she knew she could ask anything, but she wanted to be asked, she wanted to be praised. She needed to know that it had felt good that it had been alright. She was a little worried that her body would go that one step further and she might find herself married and pregnant. She had no doubt that he would marry her.

Harold lay there enjoying the high that had come from their sexual pursuits and just quietly to himself he noted how he would have liked a scotch at this point. He hadn't known she was a virgin, indeed he had never given it any consideration. whether it was her speaking of Phylis that had thrown him off the scent he did not know. But there was something about taking a virgin that was unique. To be the first, to know it as untouched, to take her as a child, albeit an adult. That little purse that would know love for the first time.

Eventually Harold slipped off to sleep, Charlotte by his side watching as his eyes became heavier and his conversation lapsed. But she woke again in the small hours of the morning, Harold was talking in his sleep and talking quite loudly. At first she could not make out what he was saying but as she came round it began making a little more sense. He was speaking to somebody, he could not find someone, no that person was not there, you'll go to the devil not I, and the like. Then from speaking to himself he went into a heavy cold sweat, his head thrashed from side to side and his body vibrated. Fearing for herself Charlotte woke him and he was soon quiet again.
"You were talking in your sleep," she said.
"Was I?" He replied, now as docile as a lamb. She had expected him to wake as he had been in sleep but the contrary could not have been more the case.
"I don't know what you were saying," she reassured him.
"What time is it?"
"I think it is a little before dawn, if you go over to the window you may be able to tell."
"Too cold." And he made as if to shiver, for although it was certainly not the sort of weather when one needed a fire set in the grate, there had been little cloud cover and the air was

fresh to say the least.
"I would much rather stay with you." He continued.
"Well look, you can just see between the curtains it is not yet just first light."
"I'm sorry but to me it looks like the dead of night. What did you wake me for?"
"Oh silly, you know what I woke you for?"
"Ah yes I was having a nightmare."
"I did not say that."
"Perhaps not but I think I was. It's far too early to get up so I suppose we will just have to lie here until Morning comes. I can't help feeling a touch on the hungry side even so. It's moments like this one wishes one was at home when one could go down and raid the pantry."
He had made her laugh although they were both aware that this time of night was not the sort of time to be making fun.

"I don't know I think I might get dressed and have a walk along the quayside, if I let myself out quietly I cannot see why anyone would worry. It's not like I'm running off without paying. I don't know whether you want to stay here and try and sleep a bit more or perhaps you might like to read. You understand it is not that I don't want you to come with me, but I've a feeling today, may turn out to be a very long day indeed. But by all means come with me if you want to."

Charlotte had got the general drift of things, he wanted some time for himself, and who was she to deny him that. Truth be told she could have done with some herself and so she opted to stay and look after the room.

As Harold slipped out of the Inn, he was only too aware of how angry the publican would be if he came down and found the door unbolted. Harold could almost hear him saying, "you left my door on the latch, anyone could have broken in and murdered us in our beds." In truth it was not that Harold did not care, but at the same time provoking the landlord's anger carried little weight with him either. They were not going to stay a second night, pressing on for Monmouth as they would that day.

At the same time Charlotte locked the bedroom door and

threw herself upon the bed in a fit of tears. She did not know why she was crying. She did not know whether they were tears of joy or anguish but her emotions had welled up and now they over flowed. Then she caught herself, these tears had no place for an adult like herself, she would not weep over him. Then she started crying again.

Harold made his way along the quay, the tall ships gave an almost ghostly appearance, everything was quiet, everything was still. He began whistling as much out of habit as necessity. He dreamed of a life at sea, of exploring far off lands and the vagaries of tenure. As if to stop him thnking any further he came across a man sat near the capstan on board one of these huge ships.

"Halloa," cried out the man.
"Halloa," replied our Harold. "Can I come aboard?"
"Why to be sure, though there's not another creature about in the dead of night."
This other man had a swarthy tanned look about him which might have made him look older than he otherwise would have. He had grey hair that traced down from under his hat towards his shoulders. His hat was of the three cornered variety and he wore a long coat that when he stood up stretched down to his knees.

"Harold Banks," said he, putting out his hand to form part of an introduction. The other first wiping his hand in his coat took that hand and introduced himself as Jack.
"So what brings a young gentleman like yourself out in the dead of night? I take it you won't be joining the crew or running away."
"No, I couldn't sleep and decided I needed some air. Nothing anymore capricious than that."
"Now there's a word and at this time of night. I tell he knows my sense, like as not. But you are not alone, is it? And you didn't come all this way just to see your humble friend Jack. As like or not it would be a woman? Am I right?"
Had Harold been of more years than he had he would undoubtedly have been most affronted by this seeming breach of the rules of privacy but he was not and hence he could not forego his curiosity.

"I don't know how you could possibly know such a thing? But there may be a glimmer of truth in that."

"Ay, you may well ask how I know? But you don't often find a young man like yourself wandering about the quayside in the dead of night if it warn't for the sake of a woman. In truth I don't know any more about you than you know of me. But I fancy there is loving there. Indulge me if you will."

"I think you know very well," replied Harold. "How accurate you are. And while I cannot comprehend how that should be the case, I am a little taken back at your presumed knowledge of myself."

"Come, come, Sir," continued Jack. "You and me are both men of the world. Why not share the burden of your worries? Have you got a girl in trouble? It'll go no further but then if you have an idea to keep a secret then so be it." Half way through this speech Jack had touched his nose with his finger indicating again that he suspected what he might have been saying was so.

"No, no, nothing like that. Though you would agree Charlotte is a very attractive woman."

"Oh, Charlotte is it now. Well if I may be as bold I think this Charlotte had got you caught up, but then that is not all bad." Here Jack paused he knew he now had Harold exactly where he wanted him and that the latter would now give up his confidence.

"Charlotte, how can I tell you? She is beautiful to the eye, she is educated, she is versed in the arts, she has a keen wit and yes I'm very much attracted to her."

"And yet you worry. You don't want to make her yours? Listen you ain't from these parts are you, you are west country maybe but you are not Bristolian. I've sailed the seven seas and if there ain't one thing that would break a man's heart it is a woman. Then you ain't thinking of marriage as yet?"

"Frankly I'm not at all sure my uncle would agree to it, though I suppose if it's really what I want he cannot stop me."

"Your uncle that would be your Guardian, would it?"

"But enough of me," said Harold with a sudden change of tack. "Do you sail soon?"

"Not for another three weeks, we run out towards the West

Indies." Jack evidently spoke abruptly, whatever else he wanted to discuss himself was not one of these options. And really Harold would have loved to have heard of this man's adventures at sea. When the conversation eventually lulled and it looked like the two were to part, Jack fixed Harold with his eye and said,
"Give us a shilling, lad. For showing you around the vessel." It was the sort of request that usually would have angered Harold and in his naivety he would have refused and although he was quite capable of looking after himself, being the gentle giant, he suddenly understood. With that he took a silver shilling from his pocket and handed it to Jack and with that the two parted to continue what was now the beginning of the day on their own. Jack would continue his watch and Harold, his walk along the quayside.

In Monmouth it became immediately obvious that the anonymity that the couple had held in Bristol would be at best difficult to maintain. Arriving as they did in the dying hours of the afternoon they had discussed what arrangements they might be able to make in light of their previous night of passion. Earlier Harold had angered somewhat at Charlotte's constant demand for kisses and shows of affection and had consequently breathed a sigh of relief when the stage stopped and he had been able to alight. That however in itself had not dampened his enthusiasm to spend another night in her arms.

Charlotte for her part felt she had made significant redress, not to be found wanting in subtlety, and yet to have her case heard. That she had given of herself willingly, if not wholeheartedly, and thus might she expect the same from him on a future occasion. She did not say it, but had he asked, she would have been all too ready to name the day. For a while she may have felt she had been plucked from the perils of spinsterhood, for all that, in his mind she still seemed very young, which in fact was the case for them both.

So for each of them there were reasons both good and bad why that next night might be spent together or otherwise. It was, however, Charlotte who pointed out the most compelling reason for them to take separate rooms. These folk, lying in a border town that was neither England or Wales, had a moral standing far higher than that of the city dwellers of yesterday. They would not so easily be bought off with the odd extra shilling and for her part she did not want them to think of her as his whore. Whether the moral values of such a market town were being vastly over rated I for my part do not know, but Charlotte's mind was made up. They would spend that night in separate rooms after all what was one night when he might have her for eternity.

Again it was afternoon before they would arrive in the village in which Mr. Thomas Evans was to be found. I think they had both imagined Mr. Evans to be living in some luxury understanding as they did that he was a land owner and not just that land they buttressed up against Harold's uncle's. This was however not the case and the village with the unpronounceable name, for all its quaint characteristics, boasted no more than a collection of houses that were the type of croft that had been known throughout the land in centuries past. But for all that the sense of peace and tranquillity hit you like a warm rain on a sweltering summer's day. There were of course no shops or even pub to speak of, each one a neighbour to another carried on their business in the front room, be it for the sale of a loaf of bread or a glass on which to sup. The focal point if there was one to speak of was the Methodist hall this being the one building in the village that was not lived in permanently. Having established from the owner of the dray they had taken up to the village that they were indeed in the right place, they set down.

As the two of them strolled up the one road of the village, it leading up through the valley, the peace was no more broken than by the noise of a dog or chickens or the distant baying of sheep. They took directions to the cottage of Mr. Evans and were surprised to find there were three Evans living roundabouts. But on further enquiry, which was not made any easier by the fact they wished their business to remain private, they were directed to a house up on the left of the valley. At that time of day Mr. Evans was out, leaving his wife to struggle with the brood of children that seemed to come out of every nook and quarry.

"Oh, don't you worry about them. They are just shy," she began, in a broad Welsh accent, and then admonished them in an incomprehensible Welsh. "You've come quite a way then? From Monmouth."

"Well we have actually come rather further than that," replied Charlotte. Harold for his part seemed to be in a state of shock, though I don't know whether it was the sight of all those children or the battle axe of a woman that seemed responsible for them.

"I expect you would like a cup of tea," she continued. The most junior of the clan held in one hand while she put the kettle on the stove with the other. "He won't be long. Just seeing to the sheep. In truth we did not really know when or whether to expect you, but he'll be seeing to you. Come, where are my manners, you will want to take a seat, anywhere will do?"

Charlotte and Harold, who had up until that point been standing, were not actually in a hurry to sit down, their bottoms having been well and truly bounced upon for the last two days; but felt they should not betray the woman's generosity.

When Mr. Evans did eventually turn up, he was a much smaller man than they had been expecting; he was short. The fact that he was short had seemed all the more unlikely for the size and stature of his wife, who by any account would have appeared large. Whether as a result of this union or in spite of it he seemed a most nervous quick individual. A man who made plans and then stuck to them. He shook hands with Harold and made a little nod of the head towards Charlotte, indeed in front of her he seemed a little embarrassed.

Eventually Harold found himself on the door step of the cottage, Mr. Evans was taking him to a neighbour's where he could spend the night as Mr. Evans might have put it, "Why, we cannot have you two sleeping under the same roof, it would be unlucky and that's something none of us want. Bad luck I mean."

Harold for his part was completely flummoxed he neither understood this little man or his ways, though whether he should go along with them really was not his job to decide.

The three of them, Miss Clifford, Mr. Banks and Mr. Evans, had decided to reconvene at eleven o'clock promptly, when Mr. Evans would take leisure from his duties on the farm. It appeared that Mr. Evans was fully cognitive of the reasons Harold and Charlotte had made their journey to this Welsh back water. So it was, that as he picked up a portfolio from the escritoire that was handsomely positioned opposite the fireplace, it was he that broke the ice.
"In all truth," he began. "I can't imagine why your uncle felt the need to send you personally concerning this matter?" And as he looked up the one eyebrow seemed to elevate as if to enforce the resolve of his question.
Between the lovers there was some confusion over which uncle was being referred to and hence both went to speak at the same time. But it was Charlotte who was eventually heard out, Harold being sufficient of a gentleman to allow her to finish where he did not. Until that point she had been standing with her hands loosely in front of her looking down at the papers that she had brought and put upon the front room table. It was only now that both Charlotte and Harold were invited to sit down. In the background they could hear Mrs. Evans, and the God knows how many children, labouring away, she would produce a cup of tea when the meeting was drawing to a close.

It was now that Charlotte felt she could come into her own, and in her rather forthright manner she began.
"If I am not mistaken, Mr. Evans." The invitation to call him Thomas was not forthcoming. "You have in front of you, if not the particular deeds to a piece of land that buttresses up against that of Mr. Greenbalme. That being the said piece of land that is worked by a man that is known only by the name of Jessop." Here she took a breath in order to continue and Mr. Evans interceded with,
"Yes, very definitely," almost as if he was eager to find out, what possible proposal they could have for them. As it was it was actually Harold that continued.
"As you may or may not know for years this piece of land has been an absolute bugbear to my uncle. If not solely for the reason that it sits immediately opposite the entrance of the house and is almost continually ploughed. It is then quite discernible eye sore upon the out look from the house."

Anthony Johnson

It was then again that Charlotte took it up.
"It was my uncle's intention in sending myself and Mr. Banks, that we might be able to secure the land for his uncle, Mr. Greenbalme. Indeed if you look a few pages on you will see that there is an independent evaluation of the said property."

"Well that is all very well," said Mr. Evans, feeling that at last he might be able to give his opinion on the matter.
"But," he began. "I am afraid you have come an awfully long way in vain. I could no more sell that land than I could own my own home."

"What!" Exclaimed Harold, his voice at almost feverish pitch. But before he could go any further Charlotte had put her hand upon his arm.
"You trifle with me." She said as coolly as her manner would allow.
"No, in all honesty I may not sell that land."
"It's not yours?" Ventured Harold once again, but at this point the tea arrived and for a moment there was silence.
"I am not usually given to making explanations of my deeds and actions, but since you have come so far. And quite rightly feeling that the personal touch might more naturally endure you to me. I may in this case make something of an exception."
"Please go on."
"Well, quite simply I was bequeathed this land. I wonder did it not occur to you as somehow strange that I a sheep farmer lliving here in Wales owned a piece of land down there in the West. To forgo your further curiosity the land was bequeathed me on the basis that it stay in the family for at least a further two generations. Yes, you may say how peculiar, but as I understand it the land along with other's of a similar ilk, changed hands as the result of a bet or wager. Perhaps not anything strange in that in itself, but then my great grand father, being a reformed Methodist decreed in his will that the land should not change hands again for, it is, four or five generations. For if it was to do so it would surely bring down a horrible curse.
So your trip was really in vain, I could have easily conveyed such a matter to your uncle by post."

The other two sat in front of their tea, their mouths had dropped, they were simply flabbergasted. Charlotte was the first to rally herself and stood offering a hand to Mr. Evans in suggestion that their business with him at least was now concluded. She vaguely managed to offer her thanks and suggest that the journey had not been completely fruitless and with Harold following her, like the proverbial poodle, conducted both herself and Harold from the house. Once out of the house, Harold was given to the loudest of commotion.
"Would you believe it!" He exclaimed. "Would you Adam and Eve it!"
"In truth I do not know what my uncle is going to say?"
"And neither do I!"

In truth I do not think the immensity of what they had witnessed in Mr. Evans front room, genuinely became apparent until they were safely berthed in Monmouth. It was clear that the number of nights or evenings for that matter when they could enjoy each others company unchaperoned were elapsing. Harold perhaps being more aware of that than Charlotte. It may have been that Charlotte could envisage spending a life time together while Harold tended to think no further than his next meal. With that in mind they dined at the relatively expensive restaurant that lies within the Hotel at the centre of Monmouth.

"I don't know what I'm going to say."
"You mean to Arthur?"
"He's going to be sick as a parrot. No sooner does the bane of his life appear to becoming to its natural conclusion, than the carpet seems to have been pulled from under his feet and we are back at square one."
"I think had I not been so taken aback at what Mr. Evans had to say. I should have asked whether any pressure could have been brought to bear to remove Jessop. Because from what you tell me," she continued.
"Mr. Jessop, or Jessop feels it's his own private war upon those that have, as opposed to those who have not, to make himself as obnoxious as possible."
"Steady on. I wouldn't go as far as to say that. By all means I think Jessop has scant regard for any form of authority, but I wouldn't go as far as to say he was vindictive in that."

"I'm sorry but I hold the opinion that he is exactly that. What would it cost him to refrain from ploughing that field and using it to graze sheep or the like."
"It would cost him a flock of sheep and besides when you get to know country folk, they are often afraid to change things. Believing as they do, so often, that the old ways are best."

This could have been the clearest indication that Harold might have been thinking of doing the right thing by her. She could have allowed herself the luxury of asking him whether he did see her as getting to know these country folk, but instead she bit her lip. For on the morrow they would be going to Gloucester and if she wanted to, she could take the stage from there to London. She imagined Harold had a further night in Bristol firmly in his sights but what with the bad news she had for her uncle and the fact that she was feeling a bit emotional. She hadn't made any concrete plans. She knew if the whole story of what had gone on during their travels together, came before her uncle he would probably be very angry but then on the other hand he might consider her actions with providence. As she knew only too well he usually thought of the females of the species as a lot of silly women. Silly men, no of course not.

"You will remember, won't you?"
These had been her parting words as he waved her off on the lunch time stage from Gloucester. At that point she had been fairly buoyant, having plucked up the courage, to secure his acquiescence in taking their relationship that stage further. As to what he was supposed to remember, she had wanted assurances that he would ask Arthur if he, Harold, might accept her hand. But as her chosen mode of transport rattled on towards Swindon, she became increasingly gloomy.

She asked herself whether she felt Harold would go through with it, she asked herself if she felt violated by Harold. And as the mind so often will when left to its own devices she now looked upon the darker side of what had been perpetrated, really by them both. Had Charlotte known then how things were going to work out I imagine that she could not have looked at them with any lesser sense of importunity. True she had lost her maidenhood, but to a man which she found difficulty in believing in.

Harold on his part, realising he was not now going to have the pleasure of another night with his girl, soon relaxed. Indeed he relaxed more than he had in days, his mind given to thinking of other things. On his arrival in Bristol, he pondered the logic of returning to the same establishment that he had stayed in on his previous visit and decided that he would. As the heavy oak door swung open, he was immediately greeted by a room that he had imagined was smaller than in fact it was and, with a little bravado, he sauntered up to the bar.
"Not with the wife?" The landlord almost yelled across the bar, it was obvious he recognised Harold.
"She's away visiting relatives, sick relatives, to be precise. I hope you will not be offended if I make use of your lodgings a further night?"
"For a gentleman like yourself nothing is too much trouble, although you did put the cat amongst the pigeons a bit when you left my door open in the middle of the night. What do you think we could have been murdered in our beds, murdered in our beds, I say?"
Harold could not help but think for the sort of money he had paid for the room, the Landlord had done well enough in taking the risk.
"Should you, Sir, require to go taking the air at that time again, perhaps be kind enough to inform someone."
"I'll try not to make it a habit," conceded Harold eventually.
"I can let you have the same room again, maybe even at a discount, seeing as you are unaccompanied." And with this the Landlord held up a finger to his eye and pulled down his lower eyelid.
"Course if you have a fancy to take one of the others?" Harold gestured to confirm that he did not very much mind what the outcome of this discussion was, and the landlord served him a much welcome pint. It was as if a daydream had ended.

Despite having given the publican assurances that he would not breach his security again; he would not leave them to be murdered in their beds. Harold once again slipped out of the boarding house unnoticed and soon found himself walking along the quayside. True it was a little earlier than it had been on the previous occasion, and consequently there was a bit more life about, but in general the city was still dead to the day. Unconsciously Harold had found himself walking in much the same way and on thinking about it, realised he had hoped that he might again run into Jack, whom on the previous occasion, he had been so willing to take into his confidence. But in that funny way that dock sides sometimes have, he wondered whether he was deceived into believing that the ship had in fact had a berth other than that he remembered it as having. For as he looked up on the one hand towards the cathedral and in the other direction towards St. Mary Redcliffe, it eventually dawned that the ship was not at its berth. It was in fact most probable that it had sailed out as he was feeling a bit gloomy and a bit lonely; he conceded that he would not be speaking with his ship mate on this visit.

All along the quayside, the lack of people emphasising the fact, were the trappings of a busy port. Coils of rope and barrels of every size and stature, boxes of wild fowl, and aboard the ships, sails stowed away and capstans unmanned and almost as a premonition Harold saw himself propped up against such a barrel smoking a pipe. It was true enough that for the moment he didn't generally smoke anything, it was perhaps only now that he could understand the sheer immensity of his uncle's achievement in establishing his own line of merchant men. It was now possibly that Harold understood there was so much more to life than merely inheriting ones wealth and leading a life of leisure, however much those whom were not in a position to do so, would have envied such a life. Jack was not about to share his confidences but there was something in that sea air and the ships and quayside that crytallized something in his mind. It was then as an after thought that reminded himself of Lotty and the pledge that he had made regarding her, suddenly he wished to be home and to have the security that his uncle's estate afforded him. He did not want to think about Charlotte or the promise he had made her, secretly he yearned for that farmstead and the beguiling country ways of Lillian, but dare he think such a thing. There was no mistaking it Charlotte was educated, a good deal of that city finesse had rubbed off on her, she was chic, she was pretty in her ringlet curls and her low cut evening dresses, but what was unescapable was Lillian's earthy, almost rough sexuality. In truth he knew it, he had backed himself into a hole. Taking long strides back from whence he had come, he wished to God he could put these things from his mind, but more and more Lillian's buxom brash manner impinged, nay, crowded out his mind.

Had Harold sent word ahead he was only too sure that his uncle would have despatched Mr. Brown to meet him in Bexford, but there was something of that little boy in him that made him want to arrive back under his own steam. So it was that when he alighted from the stage he sought out a stables where both he and his uncle were well known and secured a horse for the outward journey. As with so many things his good name being quite sufficient, something he had in part forgotten in the money orientated world of Bristol and his other travels. Whilst in Bexford he took the time to freshen up, and only then did it occur to him that he should not have arrived empty handed, but by then it was too late. He would arrive at the Greenbalme estate later in the afternoon and after protestations that he should have sent word he was accepted back into the house like the coming of the prodigal son. There was a fine meal on the table that evening and each and every one of the staff felt it their job to make their delight in his home coming obvious. But it was Arthur who was the first to notice Harold's reluctance to talk about the expedition he had made and thinking at first that he might merely be tired from the length of his journey, quite against his own wishes, called the evening to at an early hour.

It was at breakfast the following morning that the two would meet again and Harold could not mask his discomfort in the eyes of his uncle who knew him so well. It was almost as if the young man felt it necessary to mind his manners, and with that in mind he ate his breakfast with an attention to care that was unmerited.

It was then his uncle that was the first to relay any news beyond the pleasantries and he did so thus:
"I am sorry to have to be the bearer of bad news, for I am sure you will see it as such, but I have had to let Lillian go. I know you had a certain friendship, shall we call it that, and that you will probably be saddened at that, but I am afraid she insisted. Mr. Brown will have any further details you may require and I'm sure she would appreciate a note."

For a moment Harold faltered, and had he not had his mouth full, might have said something he might later of regretted. Having given himself time to think, he wondered how much of the relationship that Lillian and he had shared his uncle was aware of, did he know they had been lovers?
"I am sorry to hear that," he replied, with ample sincerity. In truth seeing Lillian again had in fact been foremost in his mind as he had made the final leg of his journey and he would have readily made a visit to the farm that evening, but for a simple matter of ettiquete. Arthur continued,
"She wouldn't say quite why she wished to leave," and he left the sentence unfinished, perhaps suggesting that Harold should himself know only too well what her reasons for wanting to leave were.

"Come on, son." Said Arthur clapping his hand upon Harold's shoulder.
"We can talk in the study."
It was perhaps Harold's saddened demeanour that had prompted this demonstration of affection.
"I don't think you are going to like it," continued Harold. In truth his emotions were all thrown up in the air, he knew no more why he should have been home sick than he should miss Charlotte now. On a more congenial note Arthur enquired gaily what the news was from South Wales.
"Well," Harold began tentatively. "Mr. Evans lives no more like a land owner than say your average farm labourer; he has a free holding where he farms sheep. He is what you would call a Christian man, up that way they are all either Baptist, or Methodist. I truly believe if it was within his ability to help he would do so. When we met with him it became obvious that no amount of money was going to make any difference. It would appear that his ownership of Jessop's

field is dictated by a Will that does not allow for its resale."
To any independent observer it would have been only too apparent that as Harold's words continued Arthur's temper rose; he frowned, he became red in the face.

"That is it, is it?" You mean to tell me that no entreaty you or Charlotte could make was sufficient to convince Mr. Evans to part with this land?"

"As I have said Sir, the ownership is solely dependent upon a Will, which in itself is exacting, that it does not allow for the sale of the land."

Arthur swore under his breath, in general it took quite something to make him so angry, but once his back was up then there was no telling what would happen. His voice heavily laden with a sense of sarcasm he said,

"You of course confirmed with Mr. Evans that there was no possibility of taking the land away from Jessop and explained my grievance, in respect of his ploughing this field that is so much an eye sore to me."

"In truth I do not think your grievances would have made any difference."

"You did not then?" Arthur all but shouted this, his displeasure at its height. "Christ man, was there any point in you and this Miss Clifford going all the way to South Wales, if you couldn't even take care of the business? By Gad, Mr. Boxsom will hear of this, his niece is next to useless."

Harold was stood in front of his uncle's desk looking at his feet, he could not remember the last time he had witnessed such anger in his guardian.

"It was not all her fault, sir."

"No, no. Get out of my sight before I say something I might regret."

This was not a good time for Harold to talk about his thoughts of marriage.

Whilst Harold had felt it prudent to wait for a 'good' day before approaching his uncle, he had completely underestimated the extent of Arthur's feelings concerning the matter.

"My Gad, Sir," said Arthur, throwing up his hands in disbelief. "You cannot seriously expect me to agree to your marriage to Miss Charlotte."

For Harold who had imagined that Arthur's approval was

almost to be taken for granted this was a considerable blow. "Do you think?" continued Arthur. "That I brought you up in this house, verily I saved you from the poor house, in order for you then to ask for my approval for a marriage to that trollop, that gold digger. I would have rather you had asked to marry Lillian, she maybe no more than a common milking girl, but there is at least a streak of honesty in her. Why Miss Charlotte she can see through you well enough, bowled over by her London airs and graces, falling at the first bit of skirt that comes your way. And if I allowed it I can see as well as any what would become of you, what would become of us all?"

At this point Arthur broke off, his anger and displeasure were only too plain to be seen. Eventually it was Harold that thought to gingerly break the silence.
"You will not give your consent then, Sir?"
"Ay, I will not and don't you go thinking you can fix things behind my back. For if I hear one word of this marriage, without my permission, as the fires of Hell are burning I swear I will have you cut off. You will receive not a penny and the estate, which at present you stand to inherit, will in its entirety be forteited."
Then after a pause Arthur spoke again, but more softly now, "Come do not make me say such things, it is to your advantage that I will not consider a match with Miss Clifford, and whilst you may not be able to see that now. I imagine in the passing of time, you may come to reap the benefit of the advice your old uncle may be allowed to let you profit from."

It was understood that from thence forth the subject was closed, Harold was not to think any longer about his beloved Charlotte and in making that match that one day might secure him a wife, Arthur felt his responsibility in advising the young man that more clearly. Of course that is as it ought to have been, the truth of the matter being somewhat different. If Arthur had felt that giving up Charlotte would have been easy enough once their enforced separation was accepted then he could not have been more deceived. No sooner had his uncle explained poor Harold's predicament, than he felt all the more necessary to contact, what he saw as his beloved, regardless of any intervention by Arthur.

She had a rounded figure, which meant she had a large bosom and an equally large bottom, but for all that an hour glass figure. Her cheeks were generally rosy and whilst this seemed to be more as a result of the wind and being outside a good deal, they still complimented her milky white skin. Her eyes were a deep brown.

As Harold arrived at the barn, Rosemary was already there and as he entered she ran quickly up to him. She put her hands on his face and kissed him, then she turned from him.
"I have something for thee," she said.
"Oh, what is that?" Replied Harold.
"You will have to keep it a secret and it will cost thee a tanner, after all I paid a tanner for it."
This was not strickly true, so it is that as an object or item changes from hand to hand its value increases.
"It's a letter," she said allowing a little time to pass in order for its importance to secure itself.
"From Miss Charlotte no less."
"Let me see it," urged Harold in a voice far louder than he had meant it to have been.
"Ah... my tanner."
Harold fished around in his pocket for the silver sixpence he required, and not even thinking of haggling, handed it over.
"Where did you get it?" Was Harold's next question and Rosemary told him she had bought it off the postman.
"I haven't heard or seen Charlotte since we parted in Gloucester."
"That's not what that says," remarked the fickle Rosemary.
"Indeed," said Harold glancing at the letter. "It speaks of a letter she received but a week ago or so. But I haven't written...."
"See what else she says," chimed the somewhat triumphal Rosemary.
"If I am not very mistaken she is expecting. Yes, having a baby, and it is for you to see to no less."
Harold who had the look of one that could not be more amazed, swore. With that he turned on his heels and left the barn, hence it was left unsaid what he would do to Arthur if he found he had been corresponding with her in his name.

Harold entered the main house and marched straight into

Arthur's study, he knew from the letter there must be others. He rifled the desk finding two drawers unlocked and a third fixed securely, he could have easily gone to the stables and found a tool with which to force it. But it occurred to him then and there that he could as easily confront Arthur, and take the key from his room; quite possibly it would be in his waist coat pocket, which was at the moment hung up in his wardrobe.

As Harold tore off in the direction of the stairs, he knocked one of the young female staff flying.
"Get out of my way." He shouted at her.
Later that day, the self same young woman would recant to the rest of the house hold, how she could not understand what had got into Master Harold.

As he entered Arthur's room, Arthur stirred but a little, had he been fully cogent of his faculties he might have been affronted, as it was his eyes no more than listlessly cast their gaze in Harold's direction.
"Where is it?" Exclaimed Harold and then finding it.
"You just wait old man, I'll see you later."

It goes without saying that all Miss Charlotte's correspondence was there in Arthur's desk and that he had indeed been writing to her. One might have hoped that seeing Miss Charlotte's tender words could have gone some way to placating the young man, if anything the reverse was true, his anger soared to new heights. In the haste of the moment he broke into another cupboard and retrieved a bottle of brandy.

By now the somewhat frightened house hold staff felt it necessary to avoid Harold and there were even those who voiced concerns on Arthur's behalf although that seemed slightly ridiculous. It would be true that as Harold sat drinking, what had been a passionate show of disbelief and hurt now distilled into a cold dark anger.

"Arthur had what was coming to him." The phrase went around and around Harold's brain. Before long he would once again find himself standing in Arthur's room.

"I cannot believe what you have done." Said Harold. There was no reply.
"I cannot believe you could write to Charlotte and deceive me." His voice was dead pan, almost monotonous.
"Were you going to tell me she was having a baby? Our baby. Christ speak to me."
But Arthur could not, he did not have the energy.
Harold felt a chill in the air, it was a violent chill.

He went over to Arthur's bedside and took a pillow behind his head. This he then pressed hard against Arthur's face, there was a little kicking and an eternity seemed to pass. He pressed down upon Arthur's chest with his knee, then it was done. Arthur lay silent upon the bed. Harold had murdered him.

I do not know whether it is a prerequisite or a condition, that for those who murder, their first thoughts are not those of guilt or remorse, but the sudden need for flight. The over riding sensation being that they should not be caught.

As Harold slipped out of Arthur's bedroom, the last thing he saw as he looked back, were Arthur's eyes, now lifeless, now permanently staring.

Thus it was with a shriek that Arthur's body was discovered, in the early hours of the morning, by Emily. Emily and Avril were the very best of friends, both were young waiting staff and both had a lot to thank Arthur for. So it was that as Emily began to relate what she had found in Arthur's room to the rest of the awakened house, Avril made herself scarce. Indeed it was in Harold's room that she next appeared.

"I say this," she began. Harold sat staring at the floor nursing a bottle of whisky and had not moved when she entered. "It will not be long before the whole house is awake and what you have done will be known to one and all."
Harold did not move.
"But I truly believe," she continued. "As God is my witness that Arthur would not have you hang and for this reason I ask of you, Sir. Would you leave this house now and never return? You might not get far, on the other hand you might

find your way to the New World. Who can say?"

Avril would have continued, but Harold had hauled himself to his feet and as she spoke he grabbed her by the throat and had almost lifted her off the ground.
"Don't you threaten me, girl." His voice was gruff, dirty if it may be so.
"I'm the master of this house now. Did you think I was about to throw all that away? Any more out of you and you will go the same way. Am I understood?"

At this point Avril who had been anything if not brave suddenly became acutely aware of Harold. His breath stank of whisky, his eyes bulged large inside their sockets and the look in his eye spelt terror. She could barely whimper, "No, Sir." As he put her down and she ran from that room and ran from him.

Mr. Brown had been woken and although he would do nothing until the doctor had arrived and could certify the death and the most probable cause, one of the lads had been dispatched to keep an eye on Harold. But by no means to tackle him.

When the doctor did eventually appear his findings were pretty much the same as had Mr. Browns. Arthur had asphyxiated, or more exactly suffocated, one could tell by the bluish tinge around his lips and his bulging eyes, dead men's eyes.

"By Christ," swore Mr. Brown. "I'll take whoever did this to the gallows and then some." It was then relayed to Mr. Brown, who had not been around the previous evening, how the staff had feared for their lives, such a temper Mr. Harold was in. Mr. Brown would have to take himself in hand if he was not going to go and beat the truth out of Harold there and then. As it was the sheriff had been sent for and Mr. Brown remained with the body of Arthur, biting his lip to hold back the tears, fixated with perplexity.

Harold was arrested that morning and the Sheriff and his men took him to the County gaol. He might well express his innocence but there was not a soul the country long that would have had it so. Further that he now expressed himself to be a wealthy man, for as he saw it he was now the sole owner of what was previously the Greenbalme estate. He required the very best in defence lawyers, in fact little or nothing would in all event be said in his defence and yet he would not plead guilty.

His only visitor for these three or four weeks that he remained at the gaol was in fact Avril. She would bring odd bits of food to try and supplement his diet although had Mr. Brown found out he would have been most vexed. The gaoler cared neither for Harold nor for that matter Avril, and Harold could think himself lucky the gaoler did not charge a penny to see the guilty one.

Through the little grill in his cell door, Avril begged him to confess. It would go more easily with him if he would or so she had said. If not with the magistrate then with his maker and she asked if she might read from the Bible.

Much depleted in weight, thanks to his prison diet and often delirious with lack of sleep and fever, Harold cared little what happened to him and yet he would not confess. In his own mind he would have liked to see Miss Charlotte or Lillian or even Mr. Brown the way he remembered him. So it was that his grasp upon reality began to wane, each day a little more.

After the briefest of hearings, when defence council did very little on his behalf and his accusers revelled in what they saw as the dark depravity of the man. It was decided naturally enough that he should hang.

So it was that he could pull himself up to the bars of his cell and watch the gallows being constructed. Again Avril came and begged him to confess, even at this late stage he might save himself from eternal damnation. However Harold in his own private way accepted damnation, to him damnation in the life there after was not totally inappropriate. He now cared little for the things of this life and it was only by the most exemplary stubbornness that he was able to maintain his will.

At any public hanging there are the usual revellers; indeed half the town may turn out, and while Harold would have been unable to pick them out at the back of the crowd stood Mr. Brown and Avril. However morbidly unrepentant Harold was, it was with a tear in either eye that they expressed the love they had held for this so easily corrupted boy.

The end.

www.ingramcontent.com/pod-product-compliance
Ingram Content Group UK Ltd.
Pitfield, Milton Keynes, MK11 3LW, UK
UKHW041411180426
11947UKWH00007B/55